Choral Conducting

Choral Conducting
Philosophy and Practice

Colin Durrant

ROUTLEDGE
NEW YORK AND LONDON

Published in 2003 by
Routledge
29 West 35th Street
New York, NY 10001
www.routledge-ny.com

Published in Great Britain by
Routledge
11 New Fetter Lane
London EC4P 4EE
www.routledge.uk.co

10   9   8   7   6   5   4   3   2   1

Library of Congress Cataloging-in-Publication Data

Durrant, Colin.
    Choral conducting : philosophy and practice / Colin Durrant.
        p.   cm.
    Includes bibliographical references (p.   ) and index.
    ISBN 0-415-94356-6 (hardcover : alk. paper) – ISBN 0-415-94357-4 (pbk. : alk. paper)
    1. Choral conducting.   I. Title.
MT85 .D76   2003
782.5′145–dc21   2002153870

To Claire
In memory of my mother and father

"Better try over number seventy-eight before we start, I suppose?" said William, pointing to a heap of old Christmas carol books on a side table.

"Wi' all my heart," said the choir generally.

"Number seventy-eight was always a teaser—always. I can mind him ever since I was growing up a hard boy-chap."

"But he's a good tune, and worth a mint o' practice," said Michael.

The Assembled Quire in
Under the Greenwood Tree, Thomas Hardy

CONTENTS

ACKNOWLEDGMENTS

Many people have contributed to this book. It is a result of many years as a reflective, practicing teacher and conductor, and as a human being who enjoys being with people. So I would like to thank the students who have inspired and challenged me in numerous seminars and workshops. Some of my graduate students, in particular Evangelos Himonides, whose study is featured in chapter 3, have carried out interesting and important research to which I make reference in the book. My colleagues in England at the University of Surrey Roehampton have been invaluable in their support, in particular Therees Hibbard, who has worked with me over the years on our graduate choral education program, and Joy Hill. I have profited from my visiting professorship in the School of Music at the University of Maryland, where I received valuable support and companionship from Ed Maclary, the director of choral activities. I spent many wonderful hours there in deep discussion on a whole range of topics over coffee and wine with Regina Carlow and Ron Frezzo, who are cherished and experienced high school choral directors and great friends. My appreciation goes to Graham Welch for his faith in me over many years and for his advice on particular parts of the book, and to Leon Thurman of the VoiceCare Network, who urged me to get on with writing and to whom I am indebted for assistance with chapter 2. Their work in *Bodymind and Voice* is seminal and an important influence and guide for me in this text. For technical assistance as well as support I also thank Vicky Alhadeff for her stunning photography and James Butcher and Phil Barnes for their help with the music technology.

Without the choirs I conduct, I would be nowhere. My thanks are due to all the singers I have conducted over the years. In particular,

I would like to show my appreciation of the wonderful people of Barnet Choral Society in London and the student choirs at Roehampton and Maryland for allowing me to experiment, explore, and just be me. Most of all, thanks to my wife, Claire, for giving sound advice on the text as an experienced musician and teacher, allowing me to spend time in the United States, and pouring the wine, as well as to my daughters, Chloe and Simone, for being there, putting up with me, and supporting my concerts over the years.

I

Philosophy

1

SWIMMING WITH THE TIDE

We are all born conductors and gradually lose the ability
over the rest of our lives.
—Bernard Mac Laverty, *Grace Notes*

I suppose we could say the same thing about swimming that Bernard
Laverty said about conducting. I used to pride myself on being a good
swimmer, generally confident and fast. At my regular early morning
swims at the local pool, I swam in the fast lane. I knew the other
swimmers who I could overtake and I recognized the (fewer) swimmers who would regularly and swiftly overtake me. I swam at a pace
I had established over time, knowing that I could, at my best, swim
a mile in 37 minutes, and I often competed (discreetly, you understand, as I am not a competitive person) against myself and the other
swimmers. Generally at the end of each session, the adrenaline and
pleasurable sensations were pumping through my body, as well as
my mind, because I knew that exercise has immense benefits physically and psychologically. I was "programmed" into swimming in
this way, but also programmed into a number of suspect swimming
habits.

It was not until I joined a new health club and was invited to join an
"advanced" swimmers group that I realized that there is more to swimming than just keeping pace or going as fast or for as long as you can.
First, I was surprised that Steve, the instructor, asked me to join this particular group, but it should be understood that many people of all ages
are very wary of water and do not consider themselves to be swimmers
at all. (Do you see any connections between swimming and singing yet?)

Some are afraid to put the face under water and some simply don't want to get their hair wet. Second, I was surprised (and relieved) that these sessions were not about swimming fast or racing; we were not, after all, training for the Olympics.

What Steve wanted to teach us was to be in control of our swimming through understanding our movements holistically. We concentrated on making each stroke as efficient as possible; we tried to dispense with wasted energy and concentrate the power of each stroke where it really mattered. We also looked at the whole body: stretching the back; making appropriate movement of the hips and torso; keeping the head in line with the back and under the water. I soon realized that the power of the each stroke depends on what the swimmer does under the water, not on top of it. Swiftness comes not from making a big splash, but from gliding as smoothly as possible with the energy being driven underneath.

We addressed issues such as how much the head needed to move in order to take in sufficient breath, and analyzed whether a particular style needed emphasis on the arms or the legs. Early each Tuesday morning the group of three or four swimmers was challenged in some way; some days it felt like a good workout, other days we concentrated more technically on swimming style and finesse. We were also encouraged to swim at varying speeds, breathing every two, three, four, five, or more strokes, and to spend time at the end of each session just relaxing, enjoying the water. But each time the emphasis was on feeling good, and in each session I felt I had improved on some aspect of my technique. It seemed so much more beneficial than merely pounding up and down the lane at a predetermined and consistent speed.

Now, with regular swimming sessions with the group, I was becoming an even more confident swimmer; I was not necessarily faster, but certainly more effective and efficient and, as video footage revealed, less frantic and more aesthetically pleasing in my body movement. It was after a number of these sessions and following the publication of Steve's book *The Art of Swimming*[1] that I began to connect what I had been doing in swimming with my own research and practice in conducting. Using the principles of the Alexander technique, a body movement technique developed by Frederick Matthias Alexander, Steve approached the teaching of swimming in the same way that I taught conducting to my students. Some of the Alexander principles are as appropriate to conducting as they are to swimming (indeed many musicians, actors, and other performers find the Alexander technique immensely beneficial). Just as swimming is not just about getting to the other end of the pool, so conducting is not just about getting through a piece of music. Both are concerned with people and getting the best performance from them.

Whether it is in the water or in the choral rehearsal room, people will perform better if they feel good about what they are doing, and if they feel they are building their skills through encouragement, support, and challenge.

In this book I wish to explore aspects of learning, musical encounter, and communication, examining the entire singing and conducting phenomenon (for it is a phenomenon) from a holistic standpoint. There are probably as many texts on the conducting beat patterns as, I am sure, there are on swimming strokes and styles. My intention is to deal with how singers learn and respond to choral music as well as how conductors communicate with singers through their teaching and conducting. In particular, I approach the subject in a manner that is singer-friendly, voice-healthy, and energy efficient, and that deals with the conductor in the choral rehearsal as well as in the final performance: the learning as well as the performing environment. After all, it is here that most of the important work is done. In fact, learning and looking at how we learn are a prime focus of the book.

I believe that the choral conductor can have a real impact on singing and singing development through motivating singers, developing healthy singing, improving individual and ensemble vocal quality, and enhancing singers' (*and* their own) musical understanding. I will not deal with conducting in isolation from singing or from the human element that is key to effective communication. The belief that the conductor should know about the functioning of the voice as well as the music is paramount. But also pervading the text is the belief that the conductor should know what makes people tick: what makes them learn, what motivates and sustains them. While not pretending that this book is about psychology, there are psychological issues that conductors and teachers should examine. I hope to persuade readers to delve a little into the mind. But overall I am not attempting to present the psychology of conducting, rather a philosophy of choral conducting alongside its practice.

To return to basic principles: just as swimmers need to feel comfortable in the water, so will choral conductors in the conducting situation. Conductors need to feel comfortable with moving the body in what may appear to be an abstract form. They will need to make their singers comfortable with singing. Just as the movements of the swimmer generate energy, so do the movements of the conductor; this energy is transmitted to the singers. Just as the movements of the swimmer can be refined to produce grace, speed, and relaxation, so can the movements of the conductor to produce similar characteristics in their music-making with singers. That swimmers' body movements influence their progress through the water is probably obvious to the onlooker; less obvious, perhaps, is the impact of conductors' body movements on the music created by the singers.

Research has shown that most people respond primarily to visual images or "other-than-conscious" forms of communication. Body language gives such a lot of information that is not and cannot be put into words. Those involved in teaching will know how to read a student's attitude often by means other than the spoken word. Signs are given, statements made by facial expression, the way we sit, the way arms are placed, and so on. So the nature of conductors' communication conveys messages to singers, not just the beat patterns or the verbal instructions, but facial expressions, eye contact, and numerous other-than-conscious forms of communication. Gestures can communicate messages not only about tempo, dynamics, phrase shaping, but also more subliminal messages about vocal production, timbre, and quality. The shape of conductors' hands, for example, can influence the shape of the singers' mouths and, consequently, the vocal outcomes.

Despite the importance for a conductor to understand the many elements that go into good conducting, many people who conduct, whether in churches, schools, or in the wider community, have had no formal (or informal, for that matter) training in conducting. Such a situation would be inconceivable for, say, an organist, clarinetist, or solo singer. Many people put themselves in front of singers, whether amateur or professional, with very little idea about their potential as conductors and very little vocal knowledge. One purpose of this book is to bridge this gap. A book per se cannot replace the practical teaching situation and context, but this one aims to reveal some of the issues that make a conductor effective or ineffective. It will address those issues that should be the concern of conductors of choirs in churches, local choral societies or community choirs, and especially those conducting and promoting choral and vocal activity in schools. This is not a text on conducting patterns, or on score preparation or choosing repertoire; such issues will not be ignored, as they are indeed important, but can be referenced more fully elsewhere. The implications of this book extend beyond the choral conducting activity into the wider world of musical encounter and communication.

Another aspect of the choral conducting phenomenon is much more complex and difficult to write about. There is, I believe, a spiritual dimension to our work as conductors and educators that we should not ignore. We can lift people out of their ordinary lives through their engagement with music into a realm that is often beyond the ordinary. Through beautiful singing we can confirm our beliefs, express our innermost souls, and deal with emotional issues in ways that are not possible with words.

Conductors have the capacity to enrich the lives of those they conduct; people can escape through singing and take part in something that is not mundane, earthly, or functional. It can take us beyond the stars. Music, after all, can move us, scare us, bring us together, and express what we cannot tell. It is, as the philosopher Suzanne Langer puts it, "a tonal analogue of emotive life."[2] Conductors help us to connect the creations of composers to our own lives. Through the understanding of and insight into the expressive content and dimensions of the music they are conducting, and by translating that for the people they conduct, and in turn for their audiences, conductors can affect and transform the responses and emotional lives of those who engage in the music. Wow, what a responsibility!

Conductors also have the capacity, however, to damage people physically, psychologically, and emotionally. There are, unfortunately, enough examples among professional and amateur musicians to illustrate this. An inappropriate criticism, comment, or even gesture can have lasting impression. An attitude that assumes superiority and domination may not engender warmth of feeling or a desire to make expressive and beautiful music in the performers. Conductors can induce tension and stress, big time. They can be very *un*-spiritual.

Understanding this potential is central to the belief that conductors can make a difference. I believe this wholeheartedly; otherwise I would not be writing this book, conducting choirs, or teaching people to conduct. So this is not a quick-fix, how-to text that neglects the people we conduct with all their hang-ups, self-perceptions, and emotional lives. As an educator, I wish to go from where people are; as a musician, I want to create the best; as both musician and educator, I want to enable people to create the best. But how we connect the two roles is vital. When taking over a new chamber choir recently, I suggested to the singers that, rather than me indicate the sort of sound that I wanted, we wait to see and hear what sort of sound evolved: that we *allow* the sound to evolve. By exploring and experimenting, and by varying the placements of the singers so that they listen, nurture, and refine their singing, all contribute to that evolution and thus have ownership of it. The singers then develop trust in each other and in me. I could well have stated that I wanted everyone to sing in a particular way—straight tone, no vibrato, "just like this"—which, were I a musicologist, might have been preferable. However, that might have been at the expense of creating a vibrant, expressive, and cohesive group whose members each bring their individuality to the choir, but who also have learned how to sing in a blended, focused, and expressive way and who work and sing together as a group. So, as you will see, at the beginning of the book I look at the nature of human behavior and the nature of human learning to see if there is a connection to be made for the choral conductor.

While it is clear that there are many choirs around the globe, large and small, that perform to a high standard, there is evidence that singing at local schools, churches, and communities could be improved or revitalized. There are a variety of methods and strategies for conductors to improve the singing of their choirs, some of which will be dealt with in the course of this book. One significant way to improve choral singing is undoubtedly to concentrate, in the first instance, on the conductors and teachers themselves and the knowledge and skills necessary for these people to become accepting of and effective in their roles. Let us first define the term "conductor" or at least give an operational definition. For the purposes of this book, the term will be used to refer to all those who lead, direct, or conduct singing in rehearsal and performance in any context, be it in the elementary school classroom or a large choir in an impressive concert hall. The conductor, for our purposes, moves away from the dictatorial male figure often caricatured standing on the podium with white hair (or not much) and arms madly waving about. (My apologies to all non-dictatorial, white-haired male conductors.) Some of the principles of conducting will be relevant to all contexts and situations, while others will be relevant only to specific ones. For example, part of the role of conductors is to motivate the singers; this is likely to be more challenging with adolescents in a secondary school environment than in a professional chamber choir context. However, the conductors of each will hopefully stimulate interest in the music and its performance, and, among other things, pace the rehearsals effectively to ensure that no one section of the choir spends too much time waiting while other sections are working.

The book also stems from research I have carried out in the United Kingdom, Sweden, Finland, and the United States in particular, observing effective and not-so-effective choral rehearsals, interviewing a variety of choral conductors, teaching and observing conducting classes, and being an experimental and reflective practitioner and teacher over a number of years. My own research in effective choral conducting has also involved reviewing other research studies, including studies of personality and behavior, rehearsal strategy, aspects of communication, the aesthetic dimensions of conducting, as well as methods of score preparation. I will incorporate these findings to support the points and principles being made.

Finally, the book derives essentially from practice, my own and others: reflection on successes and failures, the examination of strategies for dealing with particular problems, and to a large extent, trial and error. My own choral and conducting experience has been in schools with young children and adolescents, churches and the adult community, and, more recently, with students in higher education. Courses I have attended over the years have been invaluable in challenging my own practice and habits and allowing me the space to think and consider. Significantly, there have been a number of conductors who have inspired me to realize that choral singing provides humanity with some of the most sublime musical and emotional experiences and individual as well as collective fulfillment, and that we all ought to be striving to do it better.

The first part of the book is in a sense the philosophy; we move toward a philosophy and model of effective choral conducting. Aspects of human behavior and the human capacity for learning are addressed in chapter 2. Although this may seem somewhat scientific and technical in its approach, it will pave the way for the essential philosophy underpinning this book: namely, that it is important to take a human approach to conducting, understanding the way humans feel and learn and the impact this might have on the way teachers and conductors behave. Chapter 3 addresses the singing phenomenon, looking particularly at reasons for singing and why people seem to need to do it collectively. Chapter 4 takes a look at conductors from an historical perspective, including what people have said and written about them, while chapter 5 explores the conducting phenomenon and its relationship with and influence on singing. I will deal with conducting as musical communication from various philosophical perspectives including the type of knowing, craft skills, and human-compatible learning strategies that the effective conductor might need. At the end of chapter 6, a theoretical model is presented encompassing the philosophy of choral conducting. This first section may be seen as somewhat academic, but please give it a chance and don't skip it: I hope that it is jargon-free.

The second part of the book deals with the practical application of the philosophy. Chapter 7 analyzes aspects of rehearsing, gives examples of good and not-so-good practice, and addresses aspects of the psychology of singing and rehearsing. Chapter 8 examines the way gestures, including beat patterns, have a profound influence on singers in terms of vocal production, timbre and musical shape, and style. This includes aspects of score preparation with actual examples and some suggestions provided for effective learning. In these practical application chapters, I have consciously used musical examples, such as Mozart's *Ave verum corpus* and extracts from *Messiah*, that are both generally well known and easily available in a variety of editions. Readers are advised to make fuller reference to their own scores, as well as make connections between the points being made and other music that they might be currently rehearsing or in which they are interested. Chapter 9 addresses issues particularly relevant for conductors in schools and those dealing with voices from early years to old age—so that's probably most of us. It includes tips on how conductors can influence, for better or for worse, vocal health. Chapter 10 gives some thoughts on what might be considered in a choral conducting curriculum.

While it will be possible to read parts of this book separately, it is advisable to consider the tenor of the text in its entirety. My own approach toward musical encounter and engagement through choral conducting is holistic, in the sense that

- conducting gestures and patterns are directly related to vocal outcomes and the music's expressive character;
- our whole communication, including the language we use in rehearsals, can have a profound effect on singers' attitudes and responses to music and to themselves;
- the physical and mental well-being of the conductor plays its part in the well-being of a musical performance or the outcome of a rehearsal.

Ideally, this book will be a support for courses, long or short, in conducting, but may also be of interest to the singers who are conducted, music teachers, general educators, and interested individuals. The effectiveness of choral conducting will be measured in the rehearsal and performance outcomes of the choirs being conducted, and such effectiveness can only be developed through considered, reflective practice, which is to be encouraged. Please explore, experiment, and share with your choirs: above all, never stop learning. I only hope that this text will provide a stimulus for such consideration and reflection. So, start swimming with effective and efficient strokes and get your hair wet.

2

HUMAN LEARNING AND BEHAVIOR

I don't let schooling interfere with my education.
—Mark Twain

SURPRISING THINGS ABOUT PEOPLE

Trevor appeared to be one of life's misfits. He was a very slow and reluctant learner; he caused disruption in class by his rudeness and his unwillingness to engage in anything any teacher wanted him to do, and generally proved himself to be lacking in any practical, physical, or academic skills. He also came from a poor, uncaring family, was very overweight, and had few social graces. When it was time for music, he would barge into my room, make a beeline for the drum kit, and play it regardless of whether I had given permission to him to do so. He also came into the music room at lunchtime and other conceivably free moments to connect somehow with the music department. We eventually came to a compromise about his being in the department, when I found out that he was often cutting physical education lessons and games sessions.

One day, Trevor came in to see me with a clarinet. Somehow he had acquired this instrument (and I dread to think how!), and asked me to provide him with clarinet lessons. I didn't take his request seriously at first, because Trevor had shown little real inclination toward study of any kind, let alone music. But, after being pestered for some time, I eventually arranged for him to have lessons with one of our clarinet teachers who, I believed, might be able to deal with this difficult adolescent. I thought that this venture would last for a couple of lessons, then the novelty would wear off and Trevor would be back to normal.

For some inexplicable reason, Trevor took to the clarinet like a duck to water. Trevor and Dave, the clarinet teacher, got on like a house on fire (sorry about the mixed metaphors). Over the following weeks Trevor's progress was remarkable, to the extent that within six months I had the great pleasure of accompanying Trevor on the piano in a school concert where he played a very expressive and heartfelt performance of Acker Bilk's *Stranger on the Shore*. This was a triumph and one that was shared by the whole school. Even writing this today, I can recall the strength of emotion of that moment. What was heartbreaking, however, was that none of his family bothered to come and hear him.

So, what happened there? Why was this uncouth, difficult, and un-talented "special needs" boy able to play the clarinet with such feeling and skill? Was it something that the teacher did? Or was this evidence of some "intelligence" or potential that had been previously untapped?

HUMAN BRAIN AND HUMAN POTENTIAL: CLEVER US

We humans enjoy great capabilities for sensing, feeling, learning, cre-ating, adapting, moving, and interpreting. Our bodies are beautifully crafted and balanced to enable us to accomplish a number of repetitive and novel functions: to sense our bodies, to walk and run, and to speak. We are able to feel pain, pleasure, love and hate, remember names, and to recall and anticipate events. And we are also capable of learning highly refined actions like dancing, performing gymnastics, playing musical instruments, and singing.

We humans cannot do any of these things without the most complex organ imaginable: the human brain. Our brains are complex construc-tions that are immensely interactive with the rest of our bodies. This interaction enables us to carry out all of these capabilities and abili-ties, as well as what we refer to as remembering, thinking, calculating, analyzing, estimating, having intuitions, making decisions, inventing, overcoming problems and a host of other abilities. The human brain's processing capacities far exceed any supercomputer.[1] The nervous system consists of some 10^{12} (1,000,000,000,000) neural cells. The nerve cells that activate our human capabilities and abilities are called neurons, and our brains are estimated to have some 10^{11} (100,000,000,000) of them. There are about 900 billion glial cells in the brain that support and protect the neurons. Neurons are connected to each other in patterned ways that form highly complex networks, and these points of connec-tion between neurons are called synapses. There are estimated to be 10^{15} (1,000,000,000,000,000) synaptic connections in the normal brain, most of them in the very thin outer surface of the brain, the cerebral cortex.

Neurons are linked together in numerous patterned networks, creating massive, complex, interconnected, functional systems. They provide human beings with unique collections of capabilities and abilities. Capabilities are what we human beings can *possibly* do: our potentials for sensing, feeling, learning, and acting. Abilities are what we human beings can *actually* do. The massively interconnected neuron networks constitute our human capabilities, and, when activated in patterned ways, they enact our human abilities. So, brains are complex organs that process, categorize, interpret, and enact every sensation, thought, and action that we human beings undertake. Most of our neuron networks are formed and re-formed as we adapt to our experiences with the people, places, things, and events of the world about us. When those brain changes have taken place, we say that we have *learned*.

At birth our capabilities are rather limited, but as we grow, cycles of brain growth spurts give us gradually expanded capabilities.[2] Nevertheless, although we have capabilities, this does not necessarily mean that abilities will be learned. Abilities are learned and elaborated *only* if the people, places, things, and events in our surroundings support that learning. Our experiences, therefore, determine the extent to which our human capabilities will be converted into increasingly refined abilities.

The concept of the mind is also complex. We do not have a nonphysical mind in our bodies that governs our thinking and controls our behavior, even though this may seem to be the case. What we refer to as "mind" (perceptions, emotions, thoughts, memories, and the like) results from massive patterned physical and electrochemical events that occur inside human bodies, particularly in the brain. Some of these events *produce* what we explicitly sense, feel, learn, and do in conscious awareness, and some of them *process* what we implicitly sense, feel, learn, and do outside of our conscious awareness. So, the assumption that minds are separate from bodies is understandable, but grossly inaccurate. Brains have no use without integration with a body, and bodies cannot operate without a brain. The brain and the body together produce what we call mind, and they are completely interdependent, or, as the song goes, "you can't have one without the other."

The term "bodymind," which is used extensively in this book, expresses the interdependency of all processing parts of the human body.[3] The term has a scientific basis that is taken from the discovery that biochemical messenger molecules are produced by, circulated to, taken into, and alter the functions of the body's organs as well as the nervous, endocrine, and immune systems. These massive bodywide interactions affect our memory, learning, behavior, and emotions: hence the concept of a unity of body and mind. So our human bodyminds take in all of our experiences and process them as we make sense of our world and gain mastery of it and ourselves. This is how we learn, how we make sense of music, and how we encounter and communicate with and through it. The bodymind concept is the basis for the holistic approach to conducting and rehearsing choirs that is taken throughout this book

CONDITIONS FOR LEARNING

We will see, both from anecdotal references and research, that human bodyminds are vital elements in establishing optimum conditions for learning. Successful learning occurs only when certain anatomical and biochemical changes take place in the brain. When we successfully learn by making sense of something, or master some particular skill, a large number of our bodymind's neuron networks are reorganized as new neuron tissue is grown to form new synaptic connections. At the same time, cascades of messenger molecule networks are released in our bodyminds and our neuropsychobiological state is altered. With that change of state comes a heightened conscious awareness and what we call "pleasure sensations" or a positive feeling state. We "feel good" when we have mastered that particular challenging musical passage or have run a marathon, and that means we are more likely to do the same thing again.

However, if we learn while we are perceiving actual or potential threat to our well-being, then our neuron networks are reorganized differently, and a different array of messenger molecules become activated. A very different neuropsychobiological state then comes into our conscious awareness that we refer to as a "negative feeling state," and that means we are less likely to do the same thing again. We can probably more easily recognize the changes that occur to us when we are under threat. Typically, such changes include an increase in heart rate, blood pressure, and respiration rate, and inhibited digestive function. Also, under more extreme threat, changes in skin temperature might be indicated by cold sweats and increased blood flow to muscles that enable us to carry out a "fight, flight, or freeze" response: *fight* is where we counterthreaten or counterattack; *flight* is where we take avoidance strategies; and *freeze* is when we are tensed and demobilized with fear. I am sure many of us can recall threatening experiences, for example, being chased by a perceived attacker, such as the class bully or an animal, or perhaps at school where we were made to feel threatened by not knowing something or not being able to do a particular task. Some people are scared of water, having perhaps experienced scary sensations swimming in a pool or in the ocean during childhood; some people are terrified of dogs for a similar reason. Some people feel threatened by being asked to sing! In each of these situations the fight, flight, or freeze responses come into play. These tend to be negative responses.

Leslie Hart has investigated the workings of the brain in order to understand how people learn in "brain-compatible" ways.[4] He proposed that human brains have three innate "drives" (adapted here by Thurman):

1. To make sense of (categorize, interpret) encounters with people, places, and things, and evolving events of the perceived "world" and of sensed events inside the body
2. To protect the person from actual and potential threats to safety and well-being
3. To increase and gain mastery of personal interactions with the people, places, things, and events of the perceived "world" including one's own bodymind[5]

Hart stated that brains carry out these innate "drives" through four types of processes (also adapted by Thurman):

1. Initiate an active seeking of sensory experiences (exploration of people, places, things, and surrounding events)
2. Detect and categorize familiar and unfamiliar patterns within the sensory input, interpreting them ("making sense" or categorizing people, places, and things encountered: interpreting events and discovering how "I and the world work" and encoding them in memory)
3. Form, elaborate, and select the most appropriate available bodymind "program(s)"[6] for interacting with the people, places, things, and events that are encountered
4. Protect the person in relative safety and well-being

So it is normal for our bodyminds to seek sensory experiences that in turn activate feelings toward the world around us. Our clever bodyminds have enormous capabilities for learning and memory. We are programmed to learn for survival. In fact, it is impossible *not* to learn. But also, our bodyminds are constantly evaluating our surroundings outside our conscious awareness to ascertain whether the environment is safe and free from actual or potential threat or is actually potentially rewarding to us.

The nervous, endocrine, and immune systems are so interconnected that new and remembered experiences can affect and alter the physical and behavioral processes of our bodies. These systems influence our perceptions, feelings, memories, cognition, learning, behavior, and health. The nervous system, for example, coordinates our

1. sensory perceptions: seeing, hearing, bodily sensations, and so forth;
2. internal processing: among other things, threat-reward evalua- tion of our experiences, planning our response actions, and our verbal and nonverbal communication with other people and memory formation;
3. behavioral expression: the coordination of our movements and all interactions with other people.

The endocrine system is extensively involved in our physical growth, psychosocial behavior, and memory formation: for example, when we experience fear, apprehension, or ecstasy, as well as sexual function and reproduction. The immune system is concerned with the body's defense processes. These three systems interact with each other and with every other organ and system of the body, triggering biochemical and physio- logical changes that affect the quality of human life.

Why should this technical information on biochemical and physio- logical changes be of relevance in a text on choral conducting? Choral conducting and musical communication cannot happen without human interaction, and human-to-human interaction is the pervasive source of learning in choirs. The interactions between conductors and singers pro- duce either positive or negative emotional states, and that will influence whether or not conductors and singers will choose to continue con- ducting and singing in the future. So any form of learning—any activity humans take part in—needs responsible handling. This is particularly the concern of those intimately connected with people in teaching music and leading musical activity.

The implications from this insight and understanding of how the brain functions are wide. Educators need to understand that what we do actually affects our anatomy, biochemistry, and physiology, and, conse- quently, our health. We have the potential, therefore, to be important facilitators or inhibitors of learning. This may seem an obvious point to make in an educational text, but it is an important one. Educators can affect learning in so many ways, not only by how we verbalize or in- struct others, but also, and in particular, by our "other-than-conscious" communication. This fact is essential to the tenor of this book; we can make a difference by what we say, do, feel, act, and generally by how we communicate.

When we say what we think learning is, do we primarily talk about "cognitive" functioning in our brains? Cognitive neuroscientists have produced impressive evidence that learning is essentially an experiential phenomenon connected to the whole body including all its senses and emotional-behavioral states. Thus, what we have traditionally compartmentalized into "cognitive," "affective," and "psychomotor" learning domains (the knowing, feeling, and doing, if you like) is not only a simplistic way of looking at how we learn; it is simply not true. Because of the countless millions of interconnected neural-chemical networks throughout our bodymind, it is impossible to assume that there is a caucus of knowledge that is processed only "cognitively" by the brain with no reference to the physical body or our feelings and emotions.

HUMAN-COMPATIBLE AND HUMAN-ANTAGONISTIC LEARNING

Why we learn, when we learn, and its success is often difficult to measure. Standardized test scores[7] certainly cannot always reliably measure it; nor can a host of other mechanisms of testing used in schools or by music examination organizations. Testing instruments are often designed by politicians for political ends and, at the end of secondary schooling, to inform universities about academic potential. The *quality* of learning, however, is paramount.

Research into the neuropsychobiological sciences has shown that successful learning does not just change the part of the brain that is normally associated with cognition—the cerebral cortex—as Johnston points out in his book *Why We Feel.*[8] Learning is actually driven by the parts of bodyminds that process emotional feelings. The parts of us that process feelings include the brain's limbic system, areas within the frontal lobes of the cerebral cortex, the pituitary body (the master gland of the endocrine system), and an extensive, highly branched peripheral nerve that connects the brain with all of the glands and organs of the entire torso. That is why we talk about having "gut feelings," and, when we hear beautifully expressive music, we have a "gut reaction" to it. In addition, the parts of us that process emotional feelings are reciprocally connected with the parts that process explicit and implicit memories. The hippocampus, and its surrounding areas, receive cortically processed input from all sensory systems, and are necessary in the formation of conscious memories and act as a context "cueing" device when memories are recalled.

Feelings matter when we learn, because we get pleasurable sensations when we enjoy something, stimulating us to seek to repeat those sensations that are encoded in our memory. That is why people seek pleasurable sensations and seek to repeat them. The feelings we get, for example, when we eat good food, drink fine wine, lie in the sunshine, or engage in sexual activity stimulate us to want to do such things again. We actively seek to do these things again and again if we find them pleasurable.

But there is a big difference between "surface-pleasure" feelings and "deep-pleasure" feelings. Surface-pleasure feelings are trivial titillations, quick fixes, or immediate gratifications like fast food, fads, or "gimmick" solutions to problems that do not address root causes. True deep-pleasure sensations are more likely to be set in motion by achievement of emotionally significant goals. So when young people find school deeply pleasurable, they will be eager to return each day. When they find a subject interesting, they will be much more eager to find out more. When people find singing deeply pleasurable and fulfilling, they will be eager to repeat the activity in order to re-experience those sensations. On the other hand, if young people find schooling experiences to be often threatening or unpleasant, they will learn avoidance, countercontrol, or demobilization behaviors. Real learning takes place when people do not feel threatened but are motivated and inspired to accomplish long-term positively rewarding goals. This is what Hart and Thurman refer to as "human-compatible" learning. The psychologist Mihaly Csikszentmihalyi refers to a "flow" experience when people are intrinsically motivated and engaged in their work or activity (more on that later).

There is, therefore, a biological basis for the role of the emotions in learning and reasoning. This is the essential and core message underpinning the philosophy of this book. Fundamentally, therefore, learning should be a pleasant experience. Singing as a learning activity should also be a pleasant, non-threatening experience, and conductors and teachers have an enormous responsibility to ensure that this is so.

My role as supervising tutor in the education and training of teachers includes observing many school classes with student teachers and their school mentors. I have witnessed situations where successful learning has taken place and also, quite the opposite, where little or no learning at all took place. Though there is no blueprint or script for a successful, well-managed class lesson, there are observable traits that define and support the concept of human-compatible or human-antagonistic learning. I recall one particular class lesson in a secondary school where the teacher spent the first 10 minutes castigating the children (a class of 26 13-year-olds) as they entered the room for a music lesson. Nothing seemed right: their chatting, their behavior, even, for some of them, their attire was not good enough for the teacher. The teacher shouted at them, thus creating an unpleasant atmosphere. After the rather lengthy introduction to the lesson, the children were then expected through group work to engage in musical composition: a creative activity. There was no real interaction or discussion about the musical task; rather the children were told what to do, how to behave, and how to treat the instruments. As you can imagine, little compositional activity actually occurred during that lesson, as they were in no frame of mind to be cooperative, let alone creative. The teacher then spent time at the end criticizing their work during the lesson time. This teacher had established a "human-antagonistic" learning environment from the beginning, which was difficult to remedy in those circumstances. The children had perceived a threatening environment, and learning was prevented.

Another occurred more recently, when I watched a teacher mentoring a trainee teacher in a middle-school choral class. The trainee teacher was given two songs to prepare with the class. However, she was instructed to teach the songs through solfège, so that the children could read the solfège notation (notated as "d, r, m, f, s" etc. on a straight line with no other pitch indication) from the board. More significantly, she was specifically instructed not to use the words of the song until the children had mastered the pitches accurately. The trainee teacher felt very uncomfortable about this prescription, realizing that the children were not getting any real musical experience and understanding of the songs, their expressive character, or context. During the lesson I overheard several children quietly complaining that they did not understand "all this solfège" and asking, "why can't we use the words?" When the mentor teacher stepped out of the room to discipline a child, the trainee teacher quickly seized the opportunity and stepped out from behind the piano and conducted the song using the words. She also had a smile on her face and talked and questioned the children about the context and character of each song. The response from the class was immediately noticeable. The children (and the trainee teacher) became engaged in the music, which earlier had been at best perfunctory and totally lifeless: a pitching jigsaw puzzle rather than anything musical. The mentoring teacher was mindlessly using solfège as an end in itself rather than as a tool to enable good and musical singing. She certainly was not advocating a Julie Andrews–style approach to learning to sing, when, as Maria in *The Sound of Music*, she taught the captain's children to sing with a real sense of music while bouncing around the cities and countryside of Austria. (Mind you, they all seemed quite able to sing anyway!) I sensed that the children in this class were frustrated and felt that they couldn't do it; moreover, the trainee felt constrained and unable to bring her own musicianship and enthusiasm to the class.

Altogether, the mentoring teacher had established a "human-antagonistic" learning environment both for the class and the trainee teacher, and had, by such actions, considerably alienated the trainee.

There was frustration on all sides, including mine as observer. So little learning took place. Maria in the *The Sound of Music,* you will recall, made singing a feelingful experience; she even suggested that singing be used to lift oneself when feeling sad, singing about favorite things: "raindrops on roses and snowflakes on kittens" (or was it mittens?), for example, or when the children were frightened by a thunderstorm. She created a non-threatening environment for the children, who had become accustomed to the captain's more regimented and disciplined one. Singing could occur only when the children felt safe. They then got better at it. Some classrooms are desperately in need of Maria (as long as she doesn't make the students wear the curtains!).

In contrast, I recall a lesson in a different school where the trainee teacher immediately drew on her own enthusiasm for the music to greet the class as they entered the room. She engaged in friendly conversation and focused the children fairly swiftly on the musical task for that lesson. There was no shouting or reprimanding, but rather an atmosphere of encouragement prevailed. The children were questioned about their previous work in the music class, and ideas were shared; participation in an orderly fashion was expected and encouraged. Here, the children seemed engaged, and some creative outcomes emerged by the end of the lesson, for which the children were given positive feedback. A "human-compatible" learning environment had been established from the beginning. The children perceived a safe environment, and learning was happening. The psychologist Mihaly Csikszentmihalyi describes this as "flow"; his research revealed that a significant relationship between challenges and skills characterizes an enjoyable activity.[9] The children in this lesson were engaged in learning, developing skills, and meeting challenges, and when the teacher took their work seriously, a sense of enjoyment was evident.

Relating this more widely to the choral rehearsal situation, human-compatible learning will take place when singers' bodyminds are exposed to experiences that include varied sensory input and emotionally significant goals that result in interesting patterns to detect, gradual mastery of the music, and deep-pleasure feelings. This mastery will in turn contribute to the singers' self-esteem. The responsibility of the conductor is then to provide an environment in which these experiences can occur. Such an environment will need to be free of threat. Part of the communication skill of the conductor, particularly when dealing with the amateur and perhaps tentative singer, is to provide an encouraging, positive, and constructive atmosphere rather than a critical, negative, and destructive one. The conductor (or teacher) who takes control of a rehearsal by informing the singers only of what is wrong with their singing creates a threatening environment. In such an environment, brain processing and messenger molecules that produce unpleasant feelings may be created because of that rather negative sensory input, and ultimately singers will be unable to gain consistent mastery over the music. Consequently, both *esprit de choir* and self-esteem will take some hits.

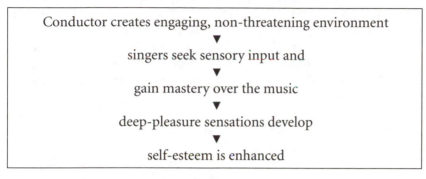

In the case of the first two classroom examples, the students were unable to seek and develop pleasurable sensations; consequently there was no acquisition of musical skills, and interest in the subject was very low. Also, the trainee teacher's mastery of particular teaching skills was not developed, and her self-esteem was certainly diminished.

MIND IN THE BODY: TENSION AND BACKACHE

A university colleague, in response to comments during a meal about her healthy appearance and loss of weight, proudly announced that she had taken part in a marathon run the week before. She had challenged herself, to the immense surprise of her son, to take on this task. This was something entirely new for her: she trained systematically over the preceding months, got herself into shape, and ran the marathon. However, it was not just the physical health benefits that were noticeable, but also her mental well-being. She had achieved something significant for someone in middle age, and pleasure sensations were buzzing around her body-mind. She clearly had the strength of character to challenge herself and meet that challenge; she sought sensory input—the pleasure sensation of achievement—and mastered the marathon run, and her self-esteem was very evident to us that evening.

The lesson to learn is that the bodymind can meet unexpected challenges with its phenomenal capabilities. In an educational context, the responsibility of the teacher is carefully to consider and set appropriate challenges that are intrinsically interesting to students and to encourage and guide students toward meeting them. The processes of meeting such challenges bring about learning, and the teacher is critical in creating a safe environment for these processes to occur. If teachers know about the workings of the bodymind, they will then have the wherewithal to bring about constructive change in young people, a vital responsibility that may make real differences—neuropsychobiologically—in all sorts of ways.

Many performing artists suffer from an array of physical problems concerning their backs, arms, necks, and shoulders. The assumption is that these are tension caused by incorrect posture or something that is being done incorrectly. My own osteopath treats actors and musicians on a regular basis. Most of these people believe that the symptom itself— that is, the pain and tension—is the problem; often this is a manifestation of a deeper issue or problem.

In an article outlining the treatment of a violinist with such problems, David Gorman describes how he worked with the violinist to dispel her belief system that was leading her to think that the painful tension in the forearm of her bowing arm was the real problem.[10] She identified the problem with the symptom and searched for ways to deal with the bowing arm or posture. The tension and pain were preventing her from playing her best in auditions and concert-hall performances where the musical outcome mattered. However, after consultation it was discovered that the symptoms did not appear when the violinist played in more informal contexts where she played just for fun. Gorman noted that although she didn't know what was happening to cause the tension she assumed she could change it "by somehow altering the body state to get rid of it."

However, trying and controlling are often negative states that interfere with the real potential for learning. In this violinist's case, the tension in the forearm was a symptom of trying to control. It had *nothing* to do with how she was using her arm, except that her arm is where she happened to feel that part of the entire coordination. It *did* have to do with her belief system, and how she was "forced" down a certain pathway of action because, in that belief system, "controlling" is the only thing that makes sense to do. Trying and controlling are born out of a history of threats to well-being—of not being "good enough" and of disappointing a parent or teacher, followed by some sort of abandonment or other unpleasant consequence. Trying and controlling are *causes* of interference with the real potential for human learning. This violinist had to develop a new construct or belief system in her bodymind to enable her to play for concerts and auditions in the same carefree manner in which she played in informal, seemingly unimportant (non-threatening) contexts.

In a similar way, we all can develop constructs or belief systems that limit how much we can convert our true capabilities into intricate abilities. I have certainly talked myself into believing that I am hopeless with practical tasks around the house, so nobody dare ask me to build or put up shelves, for example. Others convince themselves with an irrational fear of flying, or of heights. Others fear the water and believe they cannot swim; yet others have constructed belief systems that have told them they cannot sing. Whole human bodyminds have, however, enormous potential to alter these states. We already have within us capabilities we need to solve our problems and transform our lives. We just have to learn to use them.

WAYS OF LEARNING: TYPES OF LEARNERS

Though the human bodymind has vast capabilities for learning, no one formula for accessing those capabilities exists because human beings differ from one another. Each person's bodymind has been shaped by the different experiences and different environments in which he or she has been brought up, encultured, and nurtured. Therefore each human has a unique set of learning mode styles. We process knowledge of the world and our experiences in it through our senses, and all people tend to use one sense more prominently than others. For example, some perceive experiences more prominently through visual processing, while others may use the auditory sense, and yet others rely on kinesthetic processing.

Visual processors rely on heightened spatial awareness, seeing and communicating largely through visual means—drawing and pictures, for example. Auditory processors use written and spoken language extensively, and will respond more readily to verbal communications—very common in Western society and certainly in schools. Kinesthetic processors perceive the world largely through physical sensations, and communicate and express feelings more readily through bodily movement and gesture. Each human has a unique balance of these modes of perceiving people, events, and places and making sense of themselves within situations.

For many years psychologists and psychiatrists have studied the classification of human personality types according to the ways in which they perceive and process information and behave. Understanding neuroanatomy enables us to detect two "global conceptual capabilities" in normal human beings. The global conceptual ability more closely associated with the left hemisphere of the brain is evident when people analyze, search for logical sequence in phenomena, categorize, and enjoy detail and mathematical symbol systems. In musical terms, these people enjoy the analysis and technical side of music and respond accordingly. In contrast, the global conceptual ability more closely associated with the right hemisphere of the brain is when people take a more global, integrated, whole pattern approach, often non-verbal and feeling-based. In musical terms this refers to the more expressive response of the music's character, its tone colors, and climaxes.

Another system by which people's learning styles may be classified was devised by Gregorc in his book *Mind Styles*.[11] People are categorized according to cognitive capacity-abilities that they most commonly use to process information. The terms are:

Concrete-Sequential (CS)
Concrete-Random (CR)
Abstract-Sequential (AS)
Abstract-Random (AR)

"Concrete" refers to people who perceive the world in a very literal, categorical way, who are generally convergent and unambiguous, and generally need to label and sort things. "Abstract" refers to those who, by contrast, perceive the world more globally, who operate intuitively, who tend to be divergent and ambiguous, and can see and offer alternatives. "Sequential" refers to those who are planned, organized, and like sequence and logical order in things, who like predictability, and may prefer to operate with mathematical symbols. "Random," in contrast, refers to those people who interact with the world more irrationally, spontaneously, and who prefer unpredictability. These people respond more readily to artistic forms of expression and operate expressively and metaphorically.

The implications for education of these categories and learning styles are significant. I can now understand that my students or my singers might not always be able to operate, perceive, or respond to music through my conducting or teaching in the same ways I do. One of my community choir singers, Ralph, occasionally gives non-verbal and sometimes more overt verbal indications of his frustration with my rehearsals. This is especially true if I change my mind about the interpretation of a piece, its speed, or quickly move from one section to rehearse another out of sequence. When I show any sign of artistic "randomness," Ralph's frustration is compounded. Each rehearsal he meticulously marks the score; every dynamic marking, every cutoff, particularly if it is changed from the apparent intentions of the composer, is recorded in his score. He might question me as to whether a particular phrase is to be mezzo forte or mezzo piano—not that there will be a perceptual difference in practice, but he needs to know what is expected of him. Ralph likes rehearsals to start and finish on the dot and does not care for my vagaries or comments such as, "Well, I might do something different in performance, depending on the acoustics, so you will need to watch me." Ralph is a retired banker. He reached high office and was highly respected professionally. Clearly throughout his professional life, he has been accustomed to operating in an ordered, logical, and sequential manner, preferring mathematical symbols to artistic ones. He likes the technical aspects of the music, needing to get the notes right, even at the expense of the expressive character of the music. He sees the music as a technical challenge. That is not to undervalue his response to music at all, but rather to illustrate that, as teachers and conductors, we need to be aware of the differing learning styles that people have.

Another singer, at the time when the choir was learning a piece of music with a 5/8 time signature, made the suggestion that the singers should count the six beats then take away one, the assumption being that 5/8 was not a normal musical concept. The thinking behind this was a logical mathematical solution to what was perceived as a technical problem. This singer was employed to solve problems for the Ministry of Defence in London—no room for abstract randomness there! My "abstract" response to this "sequential" suggestion was to indicate that this was far too complex an approach and that 5/8 time was neither problematic nor abnormal; it merely had to be "felt."

A "concrete-sequential" tenor being conducted by an "abstract-random" conductor must be a challenge for both: where do they meet? But the obligation is on teachers and conductors to accommodate the learning needs of all their students and singers and make adjustments in practice accordingly. Any average choir, for example, will have a mixture of learning styles—CS, CR, AS, and AR—represented among its members. This has wider implications for teaching, promoting learning, and motivating students in choirs, in music classes, or in any other area of life in which human interaction takes place.

Education points us toward perceiving the world in all sorts of ways. We need the opportunities to develop human capabilities from a variety of perspectives, and that is why we all need a balanced curriculum in our schools to enable us to see and make sense of the world artistically and scientifically, logically and linguistically, from study of the humanities to engagement in physical education, and so on.

Howard Gardner has proposed multiple intelligences that encapsulate certain types of knowledge, capabilities and abilities. His original seven intelligences were

- Bodily-kinesthetic
- Visual-spatial
- Linguistic

- Musical
- Logical-mathematical
- Intrapersonal
- Interpersonal

More recently, in his book *Intelligence Reframed,* Gardner considers evidence for three further intelligences, namely "naturalistic," "spiritual," and "existential," and questions whether there might be evidence also for a distinct "moral" intelligence.[12]

Here we see that music is considered a distinct intelligence to use Gardner's term, or what we might consider to be distinct clusters of human capability and ability. This may well help to account for Trevor's success with the clarinet. By recognizing such distinct capability-ability clusters (intelligences) as, for example, "bodily-kinesthetic," "spatial," and "interpersonal" in addition to "mathematical," "linguistic," and "musical," Gardner's theory reveals that, even in Western society, people need and use a wide variety of their capabilities and abilities (intelligences) in their day-to-day living. Nevertheless, it cannot but be noticeable that most schooling is primarily concerned with the testing of logical-mathematical and linguistic abilities. We all know of students who excel in a particular field like music or sports, or are exceedingly capable in making things or communicating with people, but who also perhaps have difficulty with language or mathematics. We also know those who excel in mathematics but who have little interpersonal communication ability, for example.

SCHOOLS, EDUCATIONAL GOALS, AND STANDARDS

Most of the world's societies use schools as the prime organization in which to teach their young. Education, or to put it more accurately, schooling in much of Europe and North America today refers to "standards." Often there is a concentration on the development of literacy and numeracy as well as the collection and regurgitation of prescribed fact and formula-based knowledge. Curricula are organized usually in compartments of discrete subject areas and removed from real-life experiences. Politicians have argued that standards are not high enough and have directed schools to demonstrate academic accountability to the public. A significantly increased testing culture has resulted that assesses facts and formula-based knowledge through right-answer, easy-to-grade multiple-choice tests. Most teachers are then forced into assessment-driven curricula in order that they can be accountable to parents, governors, and politicians. To ensure high test scores, many teachers then focus on teaching to the tests; you know the phrase about fattening the pig by weighing it all the time? There is a common misconception that testing per se increases learning and that higher scores are evidence of rising standards. Testing may well be fine for those who "pass" or score highly, and it may be perfectly acceptable when publishing test scores for those schools that have performed well: but what about the schools that have low or even average test scores? What does it do for the morale of teachers and students if they are constantly told they are not up to the mark?

Human-compatible learning focuses on the *quality* of interaction between teacher and learner, on *how* learning happens, rather than on merely the academic content and the "result." The obsession with test scores raises a question: are we as teachers concerned about the learning experiences of our students as whole human beings or only the academic end result? Educational goals and standards may prescribe what is to be learned, but they do not necessarily consider the quality of the learning experience and how the interaction between learner and teacher affects learning for good or ill. Is there sufficient consideration of the learner in the setting of educational goals, that song to be learned or that concept to be understood?

In *Bodymind and Voice,* Leon Thurman asks, "What do human beings need in order to flourish, to become curious, communicative, creative, productive, life-long learners and to be altruistic toward their fellow human beings, constructively competent and socially responsible participants in a democratic society over their life span?"[13]

The next question posed will then ideally be: what is it that teachers can do to help their learners achieve those needs? And how can they accommodate the needs of the multiple and unique students who have a range of learning styles? To be curious and creative, communicative and productive satisfies the human needs for making sense of the world, social connectedness and independent competence. We are programmed to find out unless environmental experiences have stifled these dispositions. Learners will automatically make sense of their world and gain mastery of it when threat to well-being is absent and when their environment is rife with opportunities to make sense and gain mastery. When these innate needs are satisfied, then deep-pleasure physiochemical states will blossom inside the learners and that will result in their choosing to continue or to repeat the experiences that led to the sense-making and mastery-gaining.

Thurman gives examples of how we might translate explicit music learning goals or "standards" into human-compatible learning modes. He states a "content standard," a written curriculum goal for music, and within its framework moves toward spoken "pinpoint goals" where students (learners) are included in the goal-setting process. In this format, educational goals can be then formulated to take into account learners' different learning styles.

Example of Written Content Standards, Achievement Standards, Goal-Sets, and Pinpoint Goals

Content standard (written music curriculum goal): Learners will be able to expressively sing a varied repertoire of songs with basic accuracy of pitches, rhythms, word enunciation, and musical style.

Achievement standard (written learning goal): By the conclusion of today's learning experiences, learners will have increased their ability to use varied crescendi and decrescendi to sing musical phrases more expressively.

Goal-set (spoken to define a range of learning experience goals): "What do singers actually do when they sing expressively?"

Pinpoint goal (spoken to define a specific learning experience goal): "I'm going to sing that phrase two different ways. [Demonstration modeling] "Now you sing the phrase both ways and notice how they feel to you." [Singing] "Which one strikes you as being the most expressive?" [Interactions]

Pinpoint goals within the goal-set that include learners in the goal-setting process: General interactions between teachers and learners sparked by open questions. Learners imitate demonstrations of teacher saying the words of a song's first phrase ("Down by the Sally Gardens") in a number of different ways (different stresses of words, for example), and learners are invited and encouraged to respond, saying which words were expressively important to them. The learners then imitate demonstrations of the teacher singing the song's first phrase in two contrasting ways, and discusses with the learners, "Which version feels more expressive of the feeling meaning of the song?" The learners are encouraged to sing in the different ways as well. The teacher always asks for their responses.[14]

During this encounter described, learning occurred as perceptual, conceptual, and affective or value-emotive sense-making. In the folk song, the student learners perceived the demonstrated sound of different word stresses and different voice contours and then made decisions as to which version had more "feeling meaning" (value-emotive sense-making). The conceptual sense-making occurred when words were interpreted both for their literal and feeling meanings. In other words, musical perception and musical conception were taking place in the context of bringing out the affective or value-emotive reactions of the learners. Do these learning processes occur in sequence, or do they occur simultaneously? Learning in such a context takes place through imitation, exploration, and explicit goal-focused experiences.

EXTRINSIC OR INTRINSIC REWARDS (CANDY OR SOUL)

Learning and sustained interest in learning happens when humans consistently experience deep-pleasure value-emotive reactions during their learning experiences. These, remember, are physiochemical states that buzz around the bodymind. Intrinsic rewards will sustain the interest of the learner in seeking out further learning experiences: the soul rather than surface-pleasure candy (extrinsic rewards). If the learning has been intrinsically deep-pleasurable, then more learning—for learning's sake—is more likely the outcome. That is the proverbial quest and thirst for knowledge.

The cultures in which many people have grown up have presented young people with a steady diet of extrinsic rewards for desired behavior at home and in school. A new toy or candy may be promised to children if they behave according to parental wishes. Special privileges, higher social status, or a special movie may be promised in schools. Research has shown that these quick-fix candy rewards result in temporary changes of behavior, a prevention or diminishing of deep-pleasure intrinsic rewards, and a prevention or diminishing of sustained intrinsic interest in learning experiences.[15] Some extrinsic rewards are inevitable in real life, of course, but their minimalization is extremely important in favor of the intrinsic rewards of human emotional correctedness, exploration and discovery, sense-making and mastery-gaining during young people's experiences.

Csikszentmihalyi studied what enabled people to enter and remain in a state of high-interest "flow." In his research he investigated the activities of a variety of groups of people: rock climbers, composers, modern dancers, chess players, and basketball players. He discovered that the main reason these people devoted time and effort to their activities was that the experiences were rewarding in themselves—no candy needed. Respondents (173 total) in each group all rated intrinsic reasons for enjoying the activity as being more important than extrinsic ones. The rank order of reasons were:

- Enjoyment of the experience and use of skills
- The activity itself: the pattern, the action, the world it provides
- Development of personal skills

• Friendship, companionship
• Competition, measuring self against others
• Measuring self against own ideals
• Emotional release
• Prestige, regard, glamour[16]

While there were differences in the order of reasons among particular groups (basketball players valued friendship and companionship more than composers, for example), there was strong agreement overall about what determines enjoyment.

In searching for a theoretical model for enjoyment, Csikszentmihalyi suggests that some activities, in particular games, art, and rituals, appear to be designed exclusively to provide the experience of flow. He accounts for the "flow state" being:

> When a person believes that his action opportunities are too demanding for his capabilities, the resulting stress is experienced as anxiety; when the ratio of capabilities is higher, but the challenges are still too demanding for his skills, the experience is worry. The state of flow is felt when opportunities for action are in balance with the actor's skills; the experience is the autotelic. When the skills are greater than the opportunities for using them, the state of boredom results; this state again fades into anxiety when the ratio becomes too large.[17]

This has clear messages for educators: conductors as well as teachers. If we want to facilitate optimum learning, then helping our students get into a state of flow will be our aim. A state of flow is facilitated when what people are faced with doing (action opportunities) is just a bit beyond their current ability to accomplish it (a novelty effect), but their prior learning has prepared them for figuring out how to do it with some "target practice."[18] If young choral singers have been singing expressive homophonic music very skillfully and are faced with simple expressive polyphonic music, then their prior experiences have prepared them to take on the challenge of multiple simultaneous melodies. Intrinsic reward and flow involvement are then much more likely. If singers who have had little experience with sight-singing, however, are expected to sight-sing melodies a cappella, they will perceive that expectation as a considerable threat to their well-being, fairly strong unpleasant feeling will occur (anxiety), and some form of the fight, flight, or freeze behavior will occur. If singers have learned to sight-sing fairly well any music that is composed in common-practice harmony and stays in one tonality, but then they are expected to sight-sing a piece of music that modulates tonal centers frequently, they too will perceive that expectation as a threat to their well-being. Relatively mild unpleasant feelings will occur (worry) and, in many people, some form of freeze behavior will happen that is likely to result in sight-singing inaccuracies that are even more threatening to well-being (anxiety). On the other hand, if those same singers were given a steady diet of simple melodies to sight-sing, boredom might well result in disillusioned students and consequent disruptive behavior.

Singers will also feel anxious if, for example, a chosen repertoire is too demanding for their capabilities. Conversely, if the demands are less than their skills, then boredom will result and attendance and intrinsic interest in the activity may suffer. I have seen too many situations where conductors have set inappropriate music for their singers. Bach's *Mass in B minor* is a sublime work, challenging to perform by any standards, but it will not give anyone pleasure, certainly not ecstasy, if it is realistically beyond the capabilities of the singers. Also, I have witnessed school students being given repertoire that is far too undemanding (a diet of unison pop songs, for example) with the upshot that the young people do not really find the activity intrinsically rewarding as there is no challenge; skill development is nonexistent, expressive experiences do not occur, and boredom ensues.

LANGUAGE AND CONTROL

Our habitual patterns of talking in rehearsals can inhibit learning or help it blossom. The words we use can have negative or positive effects on people's willingness to cooperate and on their confidence. Threatening environments can be created very easily through language, but also they can be effortlessly created by other-than-conscious means. In fact, choral singers can become conditioned to expect that conductors are supposed to threaten them and treat them as though they cannot think for themselves.

Some time ago with my adult community choir in London, I asked the 120 members how they felt about a section we had just rehearsed. I recall the immediate and emphatic response from one of the more outspoken altos: "Well, you tell us—you're the conductor!" The implication was that they expected to be told, to be instructed and reprimanded for mistakes. They had been unaccustomed to having any input into their choral learning experiences. They had been used to being controlled by the conductor; the conductor had needed them to be under his control in order to be needed himself.

Many conductors operate by abnegating themselves from the responsibility for the musical outcome, by adopting an accusatory posture; the tuning problems, for example, are blamed on the sopranos—"you're always flat in this section!" What this really means is that the conductor or teacher is not willing to take, or at least share, the responsibility for the tuning difficulties. Blame is a negative and antagonistic strategy that is far too often used by conductors and teachers. How much more effective it would be for the conductor to make helpful suggestions as to how the tuning problems might be solved; or at least try different approaches and strategies and generate a sharing of solutions to the problem. There would then be a more cooperative ethos created—solving the problem together—in which people take partnership in the activity rather than just being told they are not good enough.

Certain words and phrases, facial expressions, and gestures communicate coercive control of the singers by the teacher or conductor; some encourage dependency on the teacher or conductor, and others suggest accusation of inadequacy by the teacher or conductor. These communications all tend to create human-antagonistic learning environments. The inset shows some common examples:

Language of Control

Don't sing like that . . .
NO!
Why can't you sing that nicely?
Do this now . . .
Watch me all the time . . .

Language of Dependency

I want you to sing this phrase . . .
I need you to give me 100 percent effort here . . .
Do this for me . . .
Give me . . .

Language of Accusation

You really aren't singing that properly at all . . .
What's wrong with you all today?
I can't understand why . . .
How many times do I have to tell you . . . ?
That's just not good enough . . .

FEEDBACK FOR HIGH-QUALITY LEARNING

People in learning situations take a "target-practice" approach toward measuring their perceived goals. Singers in choral rehearsals are constantly taking aim at the bull's-eyes of accurate pitches and rhythms of the music they are learning, singing with more and more vocal efficiency and capturing the composers' intentions in terms of expressive character and nuances. What matters to them is that each successive target practice is nearing the bull's-eye more and more. But how do they know they are nearing the bull's-eye? Leslie Hart states that the principle is simple: "a learner can improve by practice or exercises only when the learner has some way of knowing what has been executed well, and gets feedback at once."[19] He also suggests that a huge quantity of feedback, "not occasional dribbles," is needed to promote effective learning.

Feedback is vital to learning and gaining mastery. That's how learners know how close or far away they are from a goal's bull's-eye, and can point them and their teacher toward more efficient ways to get into them. Part of the teacher-conductor's job is to build into the goal-setting process a way for the learners to detect *for themselves* whether they hit the bull's-eye or if not, how close they are to it. If, for example, singing skill goals are set up as a focus on certain kinesthetic and tactile sensations during the singing of a pitch pattern or musical passage, then after the singing is done, the feedback is based on whether the sensations were sensed, or whether the sensations were closer to the bull's-eye sensations.

Conductors are themselves often programmed to look for the mistakes; that is certainly the case in some conducting situations, where conductors are programmed *only* to spot the "mistakes" in the singing—it is considered an indication of their cleverness and their musicianship. Throughout my own musical training it became apparent that conductors gained approval through the display of the acuity of their aural skills in detecting musical "errors." It was assumed that the more musical you were, the more technical mistakes you were able to detect. If conductor feedback is just about that, then we might as well go home now and watch *The Sound of Music* one more time. Maria, unlike the captain, certainly did not spend too much time reprimanding the children for their musical errors. And look what happened to them!

By far the most valuable feedback for choral singers is that perceived by the singers themselves.[20] As singers learn how to detect their own feedback, intrinsic reward is increased with that self-mastery, conductor feedback becomes less necessary (rehearsal time is saved), and emotional attachment to singing is intensified. Singers will then have their own sense of what needs to be done to get closer to the goal's bull's-eye, goal-setting becomes clearer, rehearsals become more successful and time-efficient, and the singers develop a sense of ownership in the singing group.

How can conductors help singers develop self-perceived feedback? Learning cycles begin with goal-setting and then a go at that target's bull's-eye. Then the conductor can give the singers an opportunity to bring their self-perceived feedback into conscious awareness by asking one or more questions about how the "go" went. The questions would, of course, be related to the goal at hand. "Did you notice a difference in the decrescendo that time?" "Was that rhythm closer to the bull's-eye, about the same, or further away?" "Did our tone quality seem breathy, pressed-edgy, or firm-clear-mellow-warm to you?"

Inexperienced singers and singers who have been told what they've done wrong all the time may not have a vocabulary for expressing their self-perceived feedback. Conductors, then, need to give them vocabulary models before the questions. "I heard some inaccurate pitches that time. Did you?" "I heard some pitches going flat in the bass section that time. Did you hear that, basses? What can we do?" "I heard the rhythm being just behind the beat. The vowels speak on the rhythm, not the consonants, right? Do it." "To be honest, the music didn't really move me that time. What can we do to make it more expressive?"

Conductor feedback also can confirm the growing competence of singers. "I heard a smoother, more flowing phrase that time." "That was closer to the bull's-eye that time! Do it again." "More of you are mastering the opening of your vocal tracts on the higher and louder notes. More of you are singing with balanced resonance, now. Yes!" "I was just stunned by your performance today." Notice that praise feedback, as such, was not included in any of the above examples. Conductor feedback only *described* what the conductor observed. Two forms of praise, while seeming to be positive, can actually interfere with deep-pleasure learning. Conductor-approval praise ("I like the way you sang that time" or "You sang the way I wanted you to") points a choir toward pleasing the conductor and dependence on an outside authority for feedback rather than competence-building in the singers. Gratuitous, unwarranted praise ("That was better" or "Very good") gives empty compliments and are easily perceived as fake praise. Because it does not tell the singers what they did that was better or good, no learning was possible, and it may make singers uneasy about the conductor's sincerity.

SIGNIFICANCE FOR A PHILOSOPHY AND PRACTICE OF CHORAL CONDUCTING

The job of effective choral conductors is to rehearse and conduct singers in a way that optimum preparation and performance of music happens. If that is truly the goal, then choral conductors need to know about how people learn. We need to *respect* the people we conduct and not abuse or threaten them. Exploring the skills of the conductor relates not only to getting the pitches and rhythms right. The nature and style of our interactions with singers need to be explored in depth as well because they significantly affect how people best learn and achieve. Conducting in the context of human-compatible learning is key. But before we explore choral conducting more fully, let us look at the singing phenomenon. In the same way one would expect an orchestral conductor to know at least something about orchestral instruments and how they are played, so a choral conductor might well be advised to know something about singing and the most precious musical instrument we have: the voice.

3

WHY DO PEOPLE SING?

Alas for those who never sing, but die with all their
music in them.
> —Oliver Wendell Holmes

THREE SCENARIOS

• A group of people in Ethiopia wanders across a seemingly barren desert landscape. They are essentially nomadic, having been driven from their homes by starvation; it has not rained for a long time, and war has left its scars on the people and the landscape. They have little in the way of possessions and certainly are in desperate need of water, shelter, and food. This was a picture presented to television viewers in 1984 during the Ethiopian famine. Horrifying as this scenario was, the enduring impression left with me was that, as they were walking in search of life's basic necessities, they were singing.

• A rugby match is being played in a stadium in Wales. As the tension mounts before the kickoff, the crowds in their thousands anticipate an exciting international match. As if by magic or osmosis and without an observable conductor, the great Welsh hymn *Guide Me O Thou Great Jehovah* (Arglwydd arwain trwy'r anialwch) to the tune *Cwm Rhondda* spontaneously begins; before long the whole crowd (at least the Welsh) are singing their hearts out. It creates an inspiring feeling of belonging.

• In a school playground in Sweden (but it might also have been in South Africa, England, Bolivia, Canada, Japan, and anywhere in the world where young children play together), the children are chanting. This chanting is informal and undirected, yet is integral to the

Singing in a classroom in Lebowa, South Africa.

Finnish choir performing in concert.

Young singers from Uganda.

games they are playing. It is as if they are unaware that they are engaged in a musical activity alongside the physical one.

On the surface, the question "why do people sing?" might seem a very trivial one that would require nothing more than a commonsense answer. This is because singing or vocal activity appears to be a common phenomenon across cultures of the world, suggesting that singing is a visceral human need, like eating, drinking, and sex. But why do we seem to *need* to sing? What specific powers drive human musicality? What are the differences between singing alone and singing within a group of people? Are we dealing with a biological, psychological, or, more simply, a sociological phenomenon?

What makes singing so different from other forms of music making? Is not singing just one way of making music? Many writers have referred to the uniqueness of the singing activity, stating, for example, that it has nothing to do with the essential character or quality of particular music. Rather the human voice is an agent for the emotions, the most effective means of expressing wide ranges of thoughts and feelings. Such thoughts and feelings have been part of the human condition since prelinguistic man. Expressions of anger, joy, love, tiredness, or fear can all be expressed vocally, without the use of definitive language—that is, words with defined meaning.

From the time of Plato's *Republic* to Stravinsky's *Expositions and Developments* and even more contemporary writings, innumerable writers have posited theories to explain and rationalize our musicality. In order to establish the nature of singing and its origins, we will explore the phenomenon from neuropsychobiological, social, and philosophical, historical and educational perspectives.

Biological and Psychological Perspective

Following the consideration of learning behaviors outlined in chapter 2, I use the term "neuropsychobiological" purposely to cover everything to do with the human condition. Neurology is concerned with the body's nervous system and the brain; psychology deals with the workings of the human psyche (the mind if you like); and biology asserts that the human body is an animate object. It is not merely a collection of chemical and physical materials, but rather an encompassment of the body's complex endocrine and immune systems. Therefore, a neuropsychobiological approach essentially addresses all the issues that govern the workings of the human bodymind.

In his article "Music in Relation to the Self," Anthony Storr describes biologists' beliefs regarding the arts and, notably, music.[1] The biologists' view is that for human activities to make sense, they must derive from basic animal drives. Herbert Spencer and biologist Charles Darwin formulated the two main theories of the human drive to sing. Spencer believed that singing is derived from speech, suggesting that the modulations characteristic of emotional speech gradually became detached from words and operative in their own right as melodies. Darwin, on the other hand, believed that speech was derived from music and that music was an elaboration of mating calls and therefore sexual in origin. Darwin makes connections with the natural world and the more functional calls of animals. This is validated by evidence that the vocal organs of the body are controlled by a more primitive part of the brain than is speech.

Further research has shown that vocal sound combinations emerged in Homo habilis (prelanguage humanoids) as a sort of "proto-language." Such vocal sounds were gestures that referred to particular conditions or events previously experienced and secured in the memory. Vocal sounds were a means of bringing to conscious awareness neural representations of these particular conditions or events. Over a period of some million years, these vocal sound combinations had become more complex and become encoded into an elaborate symbol system we refer to as language. Humans (by this time Homo erectus, Homo sapiens, and eventually Homo sapiens sapiens) had developed their linguistic skills by means of the growth of the prefrontal cortex of the brain and the development of the laryngeal structure and vocal tract and an increasing mastery and control over it.[2] This meant that vocal sounds became increasingly considered responses to emotional states rather than mere instinctive reactions. Even in early Homo habilis, vocal expressions were also used in conjunction with characteristic postures, gestures, and facial expressions to denote particular "affective" states. Loud yells and growls might, for example, denote feelings of anger or frustration, sobbing sounds and wailing might be associated with the feeling of grief at a death, or gentle cooing sounds might comfort a baby. All these represent characteristic affective or emotional states.

We can recognize such vocal gestures in our music today in whatever genre or style, suggesting that music is indeed integrally linked with our emotions. Anger in Western music is usually represented by loud, brash sounds: the depiction of the day of judgment in the *Dies Irae* sections of the Verdi or Berlioz *Requiem,* for example. A lament is normally characterized by downward melodic contours as found, for example, in the lamentation for a dead fisherman recorded in David Fanshawe's *African Sanctus* from Lake Kyoga, Uganda. Optimism and hope will most likely be portrayed by upward moving leaps in the melody as in the inspired "Somewhere over the Rainbow" from *The Wizard of Oz*. And there are numerous examples from a variety of musical cultures of lullabies with quiet, gentle, and often repetitive tones.

There is evidence that the brain's limbic system was well developed in Homo habilis, suggesting that vocalizations were not only a proto-language, but were also connected to "feeling" systems or affective states. This would suggest that humanoids used vocalizations to express their primitive emotional states and, after doing so, felt better.

According to the Sufi teaching of Hazrat Inayat Khan, vocal music is the highest form of the *kala*—the art of music in the East—because it is completely natural:

> [The voice] comes directly from the soul as breath, and has been brought to the surface through the medium of the mind and the vocal organs of the body. When the soul desires to express itself in voice, it first causes an activity in the mind, and the mind, by means of thought, projects finer vibrations in the mental plane. These in due course develop and run as breath through the regions of the abdomen, lungs, mouth, throat and nasal organs, causing air to vibrate all through, until they manifest on the surface as voice. The voice therefore naturally expresses the attitude of mind: whether true or false, sincere or insincere.[3]

Moving into our own times, many people use singing to express feelings. It is often used as a form of therapy. Like other art forms, singing provides a release of emotions that cannot logically be represented by definitive language, as this is usually inadequate to express deep emotions. People's emotional lives are more complex than the logical verbal language they have at their disposal. So visual art and music has been important for millions of years in enabling expression of feelings and emotions. This is certainly the case today. It has been interesting to note that, following the horrific terrorist attacks in the United States on September 11, 2001, psychologists encouraged parents and teachers to allow children to paint, write poetry, and make music to enable them to deal with the events in their own ways. Singing was used widely in religious services and memorials throughout the country to express the emotional states of people collectively and individually.

Leon Thurman refers to the part that memory and physiochemical reactions play in the creative arts:

> When memory recall occurs, summated neural "representations or images" of the people, places, things and events that were part of the original experience are reactivated. Sometimes, when memories are retrieved, human beings overtly relive or reenact the

experiences in some way. During the reliving or reenacting, a degree of the original physiochemical affective state—sometimes a considerable degree of the original—is reactivated for a period of time.[4]

And people feel better (perhaps even relieved and released?) after such a reliving or reenactment. Singing did not take away the pain of suffering, but it helped people to deal with it. Another interesting occurrence as a consequence of September 11 was described on a radio news program in the United States in latter days of 2001, soon after Afghanistan was liberated from the Taliban regime. The report was illustrating the differences in the daily lives of the people of Afghanistan since the liberation. One man told the reporter how Taliban rule had forbidden people to sing with musical instruments. On being asked if they could record him singing now, he reluctantly agreed, but only on condition that he sang with his guitar accompaniment. He simply could not, after years of enforced musical restriction, bring himself to sing unaccompanied. As he sang with his guitar in his home, other people from the village stood outside listening and eventually a large crowd gathered in what was clearly a highly emotional moment for the singer and those around him. The music obviously triggered memories of earlier times and became symbolic of those times, and it also created communal, emotionally charged feelings—physiochemical affective states—that would be very difficult to describe accurately in words.

Visual art has been used extensively throughout history to represent particular people and events. But is has also been used extensively to capture feelings associated with events: the crucifixion of Jesus Christ or the Holocaust, for example. We have also evidence from very early cave paintings in southern France that humans used painting to express feelings. Similarly, music has been and is still used to adorn worship and commemorate the dead. It appears to be very necessary to have music at such events and ceremonies, and it can act as a catalyst for bodywide physiochemical state changes produced by the endocrine and immune systems. This triggers the recall and memory of feelings associated with the event or person. In some ways it is like the adrenaline rush that people experience after some exciting occurrence or an energetic workout in the gym. It makes you feel better.

What we can refer to as bodymind processes and capacities have increased amazingly over the two million years from Homo habilis to Homo sapiens. Human inventiveness and creativity also developed not only through language in particular, but also through other intelligences such as mathematical and scientific, for example. Human capacities significantly formed and refined cultures and social structures and organizations during this time. Alongside linguistic development was the expansion in the complexity and elaboration of symbolic modes. Thus visual, auditory, and kinesthetic art forms—visual art, music, and dance in particular—became analogues of human emotional existence in symbolic (i.e., not literal) modes.

Opera and musicals are genres in which music and singing in particular play an important role in the expression of human emotions. Even with their often bizarre and incredible plots, these musical phenomena manage to re-create and convey the range of human conditions and emotions that its audiences can recognize and associate with. Indeed, Mozart's *Il Seraglio,* for example, couched in eighteenth-century musical rhetoric, testifies to issues that are still contemporary concerns of society: bravery, women's rights, good and evil, and even the relationship between Europeans and the Islamic world. Another more recent example is *West Side Story,* influenced by the theme of *Romeo and Juliet,* which deals centrally with love and exuberant urban life, but also with the emotions of anger and jealousy and their tragic consequences. These contrasting emotions are portrayed effectively in Bernstein's score by the use of tender melodies, vivacious Latin American rhythms, and other appropriate musical mechanisms to stimulate emotional responses.

Songs and singing are particularly effective ways of reproducing "feeling states" of human emotive existence. These are encoded in memory and, when songs are sung, the memory is able to recall the original feeling states and transform them into the present. So, songwriters are able to capture the feeling sense of words—being aware of the rhythmic pattern of spoken words—and recognize the expressive elements inherent in the vocal gestures in order to re-create sounds and structures that will encapsulate feelings associated with the sentiment of the song. Such sounds and structures (musical gestures) are used in patriotic songs and national anthems to re-create pride or national identity, love songs (plenty of examples there), lullabies, or songs of sorrow. The use of musical elements in the construction of songs will be salient in their capacity to reproduce or incite those feeling states. Deryck Cooke, in his book *The Language of Music,* attempted to provide a vocabulary of musical gesture to denote and reflect particular expressive intentions of instrumental as well as vocal compositions, drawing on examples from Western music from the Renaissance to the twentieth century.

I always find it interesting to analyze the ways in which composers set lines of text, sacred or secular, and there are enough fine examples of music for solo voice as well as choral. We only have to look at the songs of Purcell, Schubert, Britten, Sondheim, or Lennon and McCartney, to name a few, to find some finely composed examples of text treatment in vocal lines. The craft of composing vocal music is to be inspired by words and then capture the character and expression of those words in the composition. The solo singer then has to capture the same expression and character in the performance of the song for others (the listeners) to hear and recognize its expressive dimension. The performance, by solo voice or multiple choral voices, expresses feelings associated with the song's character. Leon Thurman suggests these are "as-if" feelings, but are most effective when presented with a whole range of other communication matter:

> When singing human beings credibly express as-if feelings, the feeling-stuff is ensymboled by the words and the music, of course, but also by the voice qualities, facial expressions, body postures and arm-hand gestures that are employed by the singers. If that kind of nonverbal expressive involvement is minimal or missing, then observers will be less able to engage empathically with the words and the music.[5]

So singing is essentially about communication; and for the substance of this book, it is about communication between conductors and singers and then singers and their listeners. Understanding the import of music's text is a fundamental issue for conductors and singers to portray those as-if feelings.

Social Perspective

Apart from having a musical function, collective singing has, undoubtedly, a social function. Humans are essentially social animals; music is essentially a social activity. The very structure and nature of the communal singing activity makes it a social phenomenon. As with team sporting activity, choral singing enables people to work together toward a common goal. People come together with others who have a common interest. People of different backgrounds, social status, and ethnicity can relate to one another through musical participation. Within these groups or social structures, people derive satisfaction from social approval and acceptance as well as from the singing itself; they can feel socially safe. So, in addition to youth choirs, church choirs, and choirs that attract particular social groupings, there are, for example, male voice choirs that originated from traditional coal mining areas and, more recently, lesbian and gay men's choirs that have emerged in a number of major cities around the world.

Also, such situations are learning environments, enabling humans to make sense of their world and their particular culture and themselves within it. Within these environments people learn from and are influenced by what the group does and thinks; in addition, we conform and do what is expected of us. In choral groups, people want to develop skills and knowledge and make music to as high a standard as they are capable of achieving. They want and *need* to get better at it. This view is supported by David Elliott in his book *Music Matters,* where he acknowledges that taking part in music making is inherently valuable, worth doing for itself and for the sake of self-growth and self-knowledge.[6] The notion of challenge is a forceful one, and the fact that people's self-esteem is enhanced when challenges are met suggests that taking part in musical activity and accepting musical challenges, as with a host of other activities and challenges, is a significant dimension of the human psyche.

Recent research carried out in Sweden, where I interviewed a number of conductors and singers, confirmed the importance of the social dimension in choirs. Sweden has a strong and enviable choral singing tradition. In fact, out of a population of 8.9 million, it is estimated that between five hundred thousand and six hundred thousand people sing in choirs—an astounding proportion! The tradition largely emanates from the churches throughout the country and from collective social groups, including workers' groups that were established during the nineteenth and early twentieth centuries. Choirs were even formed by the "non-drinking" movement in Sweden and perhaps formed respite from dark days and long winter evenings. Nowadays they range from small isolated village church choirs to the larger urban, often highly skilled choirs.

All those interviewed placed great emphasis on the social identification through singing and also referred to the importance of Swedish folk song in the maintenance of the choral singing tradition and national identity. When observing a choir rehearsal one gloomy January evening, I noticed the collective intensity of expression vocally and on people's faces when they sang a particular Swedish folk song. It clearly meant something to most of them.

A report on choir singing in Sweden by Ingemar Henningsson in 1996[7] outlined his findings that choirs have social as well as musical functions. Henningsson drew on information from questionnaires completed by 480 choir singers between the ages of 14 and 83 from across Sweden. Significant points in the report (informally translated from Swedish in discussion with Henningsson) were that choirs act as a forum for

- social groups
- training to make democratic decisions always relating to the group
- social training and activities
- personal development
- musical experience

Collective singing activity might help people to perceive and understand how they appear to others (both musically as a singer in the group and personally as a member of the particular social group). This is related to self-image. The formation of and participation in choirs could be rationalized as being driven by the human herd instinct; and it can also become the means for social unity and communal admiration for a particularly fine interpretation of a work.

Music's traditional functional values as a socializing agent and as a symbol or vehicle for expressing patriotism, religion, or fraternity are important aspects of the communal phenomenon, as shown in the Swedish example. This suggests that all humans need to express particular feelings and dispositions in various ways within a cultural and communal context. The role of music is often connected with the maintenance of cultural and social boundaries. It is interesting to notice how singing can define a cultural identity, represented by hymn singing in church, football chanting on the terraces, or folk singing at a funeral wake. This proved to be the case at the Jubilee celebrations of Britain's Queen Elizabeth in June 2002, at which thousands upon thousands of people in the vicinity of Buckingham Palace sang patriotic songs and the national anthem many times to celebrate the fiftieth year of her reign. The scenarios outlined at the beginning of the chapter are just three such examples of identification defined through singing: in the search for food, as spectators of a rugby game, and in the school playground. In each case singing was used as a bonding agent—a connecting of people.

Within particular contexts singing has varying degrees of social acceptance nevertheless. Why, for example, do sub-Saharan African people appear not to be ashamed to sing and do so readily, whereas Western people generally appear to be less confident about their vocal skills and often make excuses for their singing abilities, certainly in formal contexts? In particular, choral singing in adolescence generally has a negative perception within that cultural group. Also, why are many Western choirs populated by more women than men?

The choral music of the great Western composers of the last three or four centuries is not necessarily part of cultural traditions of all countries, and so music in schools may reflect a whole scenario of varied practice. Within short geographical distances, collective singing traditions vary. Nevertheless, in spite of differences in practice, singing exists. Whether as part of informal folk art, temple ceremonies, initiation rites, or formal concerts, collective singing is a fairly universal phenomenon.

There are often basic assumptions made about the way music operates around the world. It is easy for those immersed in Western musical culture to ignore the fact that, for example, music in most other traditions is transmitted aurally, that intonation is not an absolute concept, and that music making can be spontaneous and occur somewhere other than in the concert hall. Even in different European regions, we see distinctive practices. For example, although Greece is considered to be part of the western European world, there are many major differences, especially culturally based, that remind us of its different history and evolution. Western European culture has exercised an ongoing influence on Greek culture since the beginning of the nineteenth century, and the term "music studies" in Greece now refers to the study of Western classical music. Nevertheless, the uniqueness and distinctive nature of the Greek culture and of the patterns of everyday life suggest that the Greeks have cultural traditions and practices distinct from other Europeans.

Although they have assimilated many western European cultural elements, especially music, there is no sign of the practice of choral music in Greece, yet singing is something of vital importance to Greek people. Through singing they have preserved a tradition and culture that dates back over three millennia, during a period of Ottoman Turkish rule of four centuries (1453 until the second half of the nineteenth century), exactly parallel with the period in which Western culture flourished. Nowadays, someone in Greece could encounter the practice of Byzantine music in the Orthodox Church, popular and traditional music in the communities, as well as classical music in the concert halls and conservatories. People are going to conservatories to study Western music, to learn how to play Western instruments, to attend or perform in concerts music of Western composers. Despite all this activity, few people sing Western choral music, and the term "choir" or its equivalent does not appear to exist to any significant extent in Greek cultural life.

There are examples from around the world illustrating the role music plays in the maintenance of social structure. The ethnomusicologist John Blacking describes how the political leaders among the Merina of Malagasy used song and dance as restricted codes to suppress argument and reinforce traditional authority. He also observes that, in the apartheid days of South Africa, music was used to articulate a desire for political freedom that could not be expressed in other ways.[8]

Further examples can account for the effects of singing within a sociocultural context. Afro-American music history gives a poignant insight into the need for communal singing. As G. Oakley writes, of the 35 million to 40 million Africans involved in the slave trade to the Americas over a period of nearly three centuries, only an estimated 15 million survived the journey.[9] These people were brutally torn from their own environments, and their cultures were rapidly suppressed. Tribes were deliberately split up, their religions banned, and in some instances even their music stopped. But, amazingly, those people managed to sustain themselves during the days of slavery and overcame the difficulties by preserving their humanity that was being denied them. The singing kept on going. Indeed this need for singing grew into a new musical culture and genre that has influenced generations of musicians since. Oakley writes: "As their African heritage was stripped from them, or had withered away, whatever was imposed upon them or they embraced of their own volition was transformed into a culture of their own."

Another phenomenon of singing that has rocked the clubs, bars, and pubs around the world in more recent years, and indeed that professes to have changed people's lives, is karaoke. The somewhat bizarre sight of people standing up to emulate the singing of their favorite pop artist against an electronic backing is ubiquitous. However poor the singing is, it is still part of the identification of individuals with a culture and musical practice, or at least identifying with someone else whose singing is well known. Robert Walker points out some of the cultural idiosyncrasies of this practice with people from across the globe adopting, or imitating the adoption of the Western tuning system in their singing.[10] He asserts that different cultures use different tuning systems in their singing. The Inuit people of Arctic Canada, for example, adopt throat singing—a voiceless sound that imitates the sounds of nature and that does not depend on the pitch relationships of Western pop or classical music. While we may blanch at the sight of our friends and others singing "out of tune" in these karaoke situations, he maintains that it is not the tuning that matters; the volunteer singers are imitating the style—the acoustic characteristics of Elvis or Pavarotti—and that is the most important feature of the whole venture. The singer may imitate the glissandi, portamenti, and other distinguishing features that characterize the singing of their model, rather than accurate pitching per se. What Western (and particularly classical) culture may accept as "singing in tune" may not always be pertinent in other musical genres or even musical styles. Are pop musicians, for example, established because of their ability to sing "in tune," or because of some non-musical characteristic? Today it is media image that drives the pop singing world, as exemplified by an emphasis on promotional videos through channels like MTV; ugly people just don't win.

Walker reminds us of Florence Foster Jenkins, a rich American opera lover who gave annual recitals and in 1976 rented Carnegie Hall for her own performance of a concert of opera arias. She was in some sense an early karaoke artist. Nobody ever dared tell her that she did not sing in tune. She is especially famous for her truly out-of-tune singing of the Queen of the Night's well-known aria from Mozart's *The Magic Flute*, which is recorded for posterity. She wanted to sing like an opera diva and imitated all characteristics of opera singers except accurate tuning. And somehow, this was acceptable.

Philosophical, Historical, and Educational Perspective

The study of aesthetics has been the concern of philosophers since man has been able to contemplate nature and expressive objects. It has to do with human reactions through the senses—"feeling states," to take a literal interpretation of the Greek word *aisthetiko*. The concepts "aesthetic object," "aesthetic experience," and "aesthetic education" have been discussed and deliberated over the centuries. A number of philosophers and theorists, including Edward Hanslick and, more recently, Susanne Langer and Deryck Cooke, associate music with emotions. They promote theories defining music as the "formulation and representation of emotions, moods, mental tensions and resolutions,"[11] and composers as "bound by certain expressive laws which are analogous to those of language."[12]

Such philosophers tend to deal with aesthetic theories related to music only within the Western classical paradigm. Indeed, it would seem that aesthetic theory has been manufactured by Western philosophers. Are we to believe that people do not respond emotionally to music that is non-Western classical? Surely not! It is just that our difficulties in understanding the emotional effect of music have increased since the time when music first became something to be listened to for its own sake— again a Western trend—rather than having a specific social function. We have intellectualized music and brought it within the realms of theoretical study at schools and universities; we have often isolated it from a social and cultural context and awarded it a "disinterested aesthetic," that is, one that has no social or cultural context beyond the music itself in the studio, the concert hall, or the lonely practice room. So philosophers look at musical structures and vocabulary to explain how music has the power to bring to the surface our deepest feelings.

Educational philosophers have for some time considered that we should take part in creative activities, in response to fulfilling a basic human need. Epistemological philosophers like John Dewey (1859–1952) have advocated quality activities and experiences as tools for learning. Such activities enable us, by exploring our senses, to make sense of the human condition. We even refer to the notion of "educating our emotions," suggesting that the arts in particular have their justification and rationale hinged on this concept.

Social psychologists suggest that music has many different functions in human life and that nearly all of them are social. Most musical situations in the world are related to everyday life, to events, ceremonies, and rituals, and are integral to them as well as sometimes to dance. Indeed, in some cultures, music and dance are as one with no word to distinguish them. Within some cultures, there is often no concept of performance; rather music making just happens.

The terms "aesthetic," "aesthetics," and "aesthetic education" are closely associated with our understanding of and response to music, though Bennett Reimer[13] and David Elliott,[14] for example, adopt differing views on their role in music education. We cannot assume that all musics in the world are intentionally aesthetic, as they have social functions that do not rely on a notion of beauty or emotional response. Nevertheless, we should appreciate that people *do* respond to music aesthetically and take part in singing in particular because of its immense potential to stir emotions and encapsulate feelings. And this happens all around the world in a host of differing musical genres and styles.

Collective singing—choral singing if you like—has been a human phenomenon since ancient civilizations. If we examine ancient traditions, we find that divine messages were revealed through song, as shown, for example, in the Psalms of David, the Song of Solomon, the *Gathas* of Zoroaster, and the *Gita* of Krishna. Choral singing was considered important in ancient Greece as part of its civilian, cultural, and educational life, a marked contrast with the situation in Greece today. Indeed, music was an integral part of the school curriculum and awarded equivalent standing to mathematics. Pythagoras believed that mathematical laws and principles governed music in the same way they governed all aspects of the universe, and that understanding music was dependent on understanding its mathematical proportions. In Athens, in particular in about 500 B.C. the arts were taught in schools, and Greek students studied instrumental and vocal music. Choirs were formed as they were required for religious ceremonies, rituals, and feasts; also, choir competitions were often held. Choral singers became increasingly professional in status for the purposes of these competitions, which in turn negatively influenced amateur involvement in music making.

In the fourth century B.C., Plato believed in the education and preparation of the whole person; in this regard music alongside gymnastics was considered an essential component of an educational system. Music, he believed, could influence people's behavior, and its proper use in education could bring about good and responsible citizens. But it was developed as an intellectual subject rather than an expressive one, with the study of harmonics and acoustics being given precedence in schools and higher education. Aristotle had a slightly different slant on music and its value in education. He perceived music as an important subject to enable people to use their leisure time intelligently and effectively, leisure being considered as essential as work for the development of the whole person.

Although the decline of the ancient civilizations brought about a concomitant general decline of education, music and singing were nevertheless still given importance in the Middle Ages because of their role in church services. The fourth to sixth centuries A.D. saw the rise of *scholae cantorum* (singing schools) throughout Europe. In the Americas as well, choral singing developed in the cathedrals and churches, particularly in the Andean regions, which had been opened to the influence of European music by the Spanish in the sixteenth century. Other immigrants to America over the ensuing centuries brought with them their musical traditions, usually church based, that were extensively and instructionally used in schools as well as in their religious services and communities. Sects like Moravians, Lutherans, Mennonites, and Amish were to have a strong influence on the singing life of America, in addition to the Catholic and Anglican traditions and influences.

Outside the immediate influence of the church, choral societies or singing clubs grew throughout Europe and North America during the eighteenth and nineteenth centuries. In some communities, the choral societies exerted influence on schools to provide singing in the curriculum. This then would supply the choral societies with trained singers and ensure their continuation. Singing societies grew gradually in North America from the early days of the eighteenth century in Massachusetts and the East Coast throughout the nineteenth century. A parallel growth in Europe, particularly in England and Germany, occurred with a concentration on the performances of the large-scale oratorios of Handel, Haydn, and, later, Mendelssohn. Most of these choral societies were set up for the promotion and love of sacred choral music. Today these kinds of choirs have continued; many local communities in Europe and North America and also the New World have choirs, though perhaps not for the promotion of sacred music specifically. Small choirs are extensive in Finland, Sweden, and Denmark, and although they are often formed from and based upon church choirs, they are not exclusively concerned with the performance of sacred music. Also, choirs have developed in the latter half of the twentieth century in countries of the Far East like Taiwan, Japan, and South Korea, where Western classical music has cultural and social caché. Having been involved myself in choral conducting courses in South Korea, it is interesting to witness how European sacred choral music is absorbed easily and readily into their culture and everyday life.

For those people who do so, singing in community choirs is an important, even central part of their lives. Many people who sing cannot imagine doing without it. In my own community choir I have been amazed at how many people have indicated to me that the Wednesday evening rehearsal is the activity they most look forward to in the week— an awesome responsibility for the conductor! So, while the principles underpinning the aims of community choirs may have altered over the centuries, people still come together to sing.

Two Research Studies

One of my graduate students carried out some interesting research a few years ago on adults' perceptions of their singing abilities and their attitudes towards their own choral singing experiences in schools, secondary in particular.[15] Did they remember and regard their school singing experiences positively or negatively? She surveyed, through a series of structured interviews, a random sample of the public in various locations in an English town. Some 80 people were interviewed with questions designed to supply as much data as possible within a time limitation, bearing in mind the dependence on the goodwill of these "random" people. (Some people were stopped and interviewed outside a supermarket, for example, so care with time needed to be taken; too much time spent would defrost their frozen food, because this survey took place in August.) Equal numbers of men and women were used in the survey to see if there was any notable difference in attitudes between them. Questions ranged from ones about personal listening habits to the recall of specific songs sung at school. What was heartening in the results was that there was evident respect for singing and its place in the school curriculum. All respondents regarded singing as inherently worthwhile, with many citing gaining personal confidence and building a sense of corporate identity as two outcomes of their involvement with singing. What was also interesting and significant was that many thought that they would have benefited from vocal training and development rather than just having a sing-along. This response does endorse the theories of the necessity of high-quality feedback referred to in chapter 2, and that will be expanded upon in successive chapters, to promote the concept of vocal learning.

Another graduate student of mine carried out a case study of a London choral society (a community choir of 120 singers), and his findings reveal some interesting facts that largely confirm the ideas advanced in this chapter.[16] His data showed that the majority of singers in the non-auditioned choir had experienced well-being from being introduced to other people and forming friendships as well as increasing their musical skill and knowledge. In the questionnaires, the noteworthy words and phrases used by the singers to indicate why they remained singing members of the society included: "enjoyment," "making friends," "socializing," "broadening musical knowledge," "exhilarating," "uplifting," "relaxation," "challenge of performances and repertoire," and "sense of achievement."

During the nine-month period of observation, one noticeable feature was that the social and emotional aspects of the singing phenomenon were considered important to the members of the choir. People appeared to seek social identity within the group as much as musical identity (which also compares and accords with the situation described by the singers interviewed in Sweden). The members, with a small number of exceptions, regarded themselves as more or less musically on the same level. While many of the singers in the choir had already had singing experience either in their youth or currently elsewhere, membership had nevertheless prompted some of them to seek further singing experience either through joining other choirs or taking singing lessons. Some of the singers even gathered together informally at other times in the week between rehearsals to practice their parts. The sociability of the choir meant that nobody felt out of place because of a lack of musical experience or confidence in singing.

Data collected revealed that this particular choir consisted of people of a largely (though not exclusively) similar ethnicity, socioeconomic status, and education; their ages, with a few in their twenties and one member in his eighties, were predominantly in the 45–70 range. This would seem to confirm that people gather in groups where they feel comfortable socially as well as (in this case) musically. Also noticeable was the fact that the members of the choir in interviews and questionnaires readily referred to ways in which singing addressed their emotional needs. Indeed, the very term "choral society"—one used widely in the United Kingdom—may itself be significant and thereby validated.

COLLECTIVE SINGING: FULFILLING A BASIC HUMAN NEED

Besides the cultural and sociological differences in each case, the belief is that collective singing is, after all, a basic human need. The diversity of practice of this human need in each cultural context should not be perceived as a distinct differentiation of the actual phenomenon, but as the proof that the need for collective singing is strongly related to the culture itself. All people need to eat in order to live, but it is quite unlikely that a dish of woodworms would interest the average European, whereas an Australian native, for example, might consider it a delicacy. People need to sing, whether they are English choristers joining to sing a Western requiem mass in a concert or liturgical context, the pearl divers of Bahrain singing their songs, or Buddhist monks chanting in Tibet.

They enjoy being among similar people and using the most versatile and complete musical instrument: the voice.

In analysis of the nature of aesthetic experience and with reference to involvement in music making, Bennett Reimer states:

> The power of such experience is so great and its satisfactions so deep that those who have shared it are likely to be changed fundamentally in their relation to music. For such people music inevitably becomes a source of some of life's deepest rewards. This is no small matter, given the universal need for such satisfaction and its rarity in human life.[17]

As long ago as 1588, William Byrd in his *Preface to Psalms, Sonnets and Songs* wrote:

Reasons briefly set down by th'auctor, to perswade every one to learne to sing.

First it is a knowledge easely taught, and quickly learned where there is a good Master and an apt Scoller.
2. *The exercise of singing is delightfull to Nature & good to preserve the health of Man.*
3. *It doth strengthen all the parts of the brest, & doth open the pipes.*
4. *It is a singuler good remedie for a stutting & stammering in the speech.*
5. *It is the best meanes to procure a perfect pronunciation & to make a good Orator.*
6. *It is the onely way to know where Nature hath bestowed the benefit of a good voyce: which guift is so rare, as there is not one among a thousand, that hath it: and in many, that excellent guift is lost, because they want Art to expresse Nature.*
7. *There is not any Musicke of Instruments whatsoever, comparable to that which is made of the voyces of Men, where the voyces are good, and the same well sorted and ordered.*
8. *The better the voyce is, the meeter it is to honour and serve God there-with: and the voyce of man is chiefely to be imployed to that ende.*

omnis spiritus laudet Dominum

Since singing is so good a thing,
I wish all men would learne to sing.

Byrd was a remarkable English composer and Master of Music at the Chapel Royals under Queen Elizabeth I. He refers in his preface to the ways in which singing benefits health and well-being as well as commenting on its potential expressive qualities.

The eighteenth-century German critic, composer, and conductor Johann Adam Hiller spent much time and energy on promoting and improving the quality of singing in Germany, taking as his inspiration the singing traditions and practices of Italy. In his small treatise on vocal performance, Hiller outlines some of his beliefs with regard to quality singing:

> A beautiful voice is a glorious gift of our gracious Creator, and it would show little gratitude were we not to attempt to use it in the best possible way to praise Him and, at the same time, to bring joy to others. Those who never had the opportunity to receive proper instruction in music, particularly in the art of singing, are to be pitied but not reproached. This does not hold true for those who have wasted the opportunity out of carelessness, laziness, or disdain.

Hiller also gives further advice on the use and misuse of the voice:

> Young students of singing, both male and female, especially those with a wide chest range, cannot be cautioned enough against the dangerous practice of trying to force their highest tones, as they will not only lose their voices but do harm to their bodies and health as well. One good tone in the low register is worth more than two in the high register when they sound like a piping bird. The admiration which is paid to those who do sing very high should be ignored. Moving and pleasing is a more noble goal than arousing admiration.[18]

This, of course, might well be salutary advice even for today's choral conductor! Certainly we will be addressing aspects of vocal health and the responsibilities of the conductor in this respect later.

More than one hundred years later in a totally different context, Siegfried Sassoon wrote the poem *Everyone Sang*, made particularly poignant as it was written in April 1919, in the aftermath of the human catastrophe of the First World War. Do read it: the poem speaks for itself and needs no further explanation, except to point out that it somehow consolidates all the philosophical, psychological, and sociological perspectives outlined in this chapter, concluding with this line: "the singing will never be done."

4

THE ROLE OF THE CONDUCTOR

Only connect.
　　　　　—E. M. Forster

Drawn by Chloe Durrant.

What is it that actually happens between conductors and singers? Why is it that some conductors are able to establish a kind of dynamic interaction? Many conductors are easily able to engage their singers, to persuade them of the intrinsic value of the music being performed; they are able to give their singers, and through them their audiences, insight into the expressive character of the music, and to provide the wherewithal for aesthetic response. Some conductors *connect*. This dynamic interaction, this connection is the stuff of the phenomenon of conducting.

Is this phenomenon just a mystery, as some well-known conductors would have us believe, or is it something that we can deconstruct and analyze? There is indeed something mystical and magical about music and there are moments when the magic is clearly the result of that combination of good music, effective interpretation, and a host of other variables that connect together to make special moments. We can, I am sure, all recall some of those moments in time and place. A poignant example for me is the recollection of being conducted by Benjamin Britten as a student singing in a performance of Mozart's *Requiem*. I vividly recall in particular the final movement, the driving rhythmic momentum that was characteristic of Britten's interpretations, the climax of the fugal *Cum sanctis tuis* and the just longer-than-expected pause before the final cadence. The other-than-musical circumstances all contributed to this special moment as well (it was a live broadcast on the BBC World Service), the venue (the beautiful Snape Maltings Concert Hall in the middle of the Suffolk marshes in East Anglia), even the fact that I thought I had fallen in love . . . But it was essentially the wonderful music and the inspired conducting that made every connection for me and, I suspect, for a great many people who performed in or listened to that performance.

So, let me try to dissect, to deconstruct some of the aspects of this phenomenon. From the start we should understand that singing happens. It happens and will continue to happen in various contexts with or without conductors. So why do we need them? My argument is that we might be better off without conductors—particularly when a bad conductor gets the baton. The number of friends and colleagues—singers and orchestral players—who say they perform well in spite, rather than because, of the conductor is uncomfortably large. Anecdotes and amusing quips abound of musicians who feel the conductor plays a limited—or even negative—role. When a horn player in a well-known professional orchestra was asked who conducted its concert the previous evening, the reply came: "I didn't notice."

Is there a myth about the conductor's capacity to inspire and influence a musical rehearsal or performance? This chapter sets out to explore the conducting phenomenon, with the aim of defining a model of good practice. Conductors need to have specific attributes and characteristics in order to maintain healthy and effective singing in our schools, churches, and communities. Bad conductors can damage voices, demotivate, foster poor self-esteem in singers and players, and make mediocre music. They can be worse than bad politicians! But good ones? Well, that's a different story. We should keep reminding ourselves of the potential for that dynamic interaction and connection that an inspiring conductor can provide. Let us now put the conductor in some sort of historical context.

HISTORICAL PERSPECTIVE: THE NEED FOR A CONDUCTOR

The first signs of a need for a conductor became apparent in the French court of Louis XV with Lully and his "twenty-four violins." Throughout the seventeenth and eighteenth centuries performance practice varied from country to country, and, while opera in Italy and Germany was generally directed from the harpsichord, it became increasingly necessary in French opera and ballet with its rhythmic choruses and dance scenes to use a baton-director. Lully's music required some form of control mechanism, and thus he began to bang a large stick on the floor; it is alleged that his conducting stick occasionally hit his toe instead of the floor, which led to an infection and eventually caused his death. There is more reliable evidence, however, found in comments on Lully's tyrannical and egotistical behavior with his court orchestra, which may indicate the reasons for his conducting behavior. Such practice of using a baton-director, or at least someone to beat time, soon followed in Germany and Italy when it became necessary to exercise more control on large ensemble performances, in order essentially to keep a group of performers in time with one another. Headington refers to a picture of the cantor or musical director of St. Thomas's Church, Leipzig, in 1710 "wielding a paper roll in front of a group of strings, wind, organ, drums and singers."[1]

Adam Carse, a noted musicologist and writer on the development of the orchestra, has charted methods of orchestral conducting, gleaned from various original sources between 1732 and 1820.[2] The most prolific development in the art of conducting took place in the first half of the nineteenth century, whereas before the nineteenth century, in addition to composing music for the chapel, court, theater, or other establishment, the music conductor was responsible for seeing that it was properly performed. Terms *kapellmeister, maestro di cappella,* and *maître de musique* were used, *kapellmeister* being generally associated with the role of composer, which was the essential qualification for holding such a position in the eighteenth century. Throughout the eighteenth century, such position holders were composers first and directors of music second.

Separation of the roles of composer and conductor became more common between 1800 and 1850, and it became increasingly apparent during the nineteenth century that composers were not necessarily the best conductors and vice versa. Also at this time, conducting with a baton became more prevalent, suggesting that the role of composer-conductor was gradually changing and that the conductor was beginning to establish a role distinctive from the composer. The new status of the public concert also influenced this role. The qualities required of a conductor were changing and becoming increasingly involved with personality traits as well as musical attributes: "leadership, assertiveness, authority, organising ability and personality in addition to his artistic gift," suggests Carse.

THE KEYBOARD DIRECTOR

During the seventeenth and eighteenth centuries when the keyboard continuo was an integral part of music, the keyboard player, particularly if he was the composer as well, often assumed control. This was especially so in choral music, and in leading rehearsals and performances he would assume a responsibility comparable to the principal violinist-leader in instrumental music. Indeed, in well-endowed courts and churches there may well have been two harpsichords in performance: one for the continuo player and the other for the conductor. This was especially the case for opera performances at which the continuo player would be required to play the *secco* recitatives. According to Paul Lang,[3] the role of the harpsichord-conductor was to keep a check on any singer or player who got lost in the score by playing his part until he caught up. It was also his role to clarify articulation, keeping the rhythmic momentum intact especially through long held notes, and generally emphasizing the beat. Such practice, particularly prevalent in Germany during the eighteenth century, was dependent to some extent on the relationship between the keyboard-conductor and the concertmaster (violinist-leader), the latter being largely responsible for the preparation and rehearsal of the performers, while the conductor assumed ultimate direction. (This perhaps compares with the present practice of large choirs to have a chorus master whose role is to prepare the choir for the conductor, as is the case with the London Symphony Orchestra Chorus, for example.) The baroque and early classical keyboard-director usually had the musical score in front of him and was able to assume a baton-conducting role naturally, while the violinist-leader often had greater influence and control over the playing. Hence, the responsibility for the music's direction was unclear unless the composer was present.

Toward the end of the eighteenth century the conductor was moving away from the keyboard, as performances would increasingly involve the works of a variety of composers rather than just the works of the keyboard-player-composer-conductor. As composers in the late eighteenth and early nineteenth centuries no longer relied on the continuo to provide the inner harmony, the role of the keyboard-director further diminished. The principal violinist, as precursor of the baton-conductor, used the bow to conduct, the violin remaining in the hand; as the music became more complicated in terms of tempo variation and required more careful rubato phrasing, so the principal violinist played less and less and conducted more and more. The Renaissance practice of beating time with a scroll of paper on a hard surface carried on into French opera, with a time-beater standing in front of the orchestra. This apparently was a noisy business and seems to have disappeared after about 1789.

Lang refers to a number of composer-conductors who were meticulous in their requirements of players and singers. Mozart and Gluck were two such, the former "infusing his enthusiasm in both orchestra and singers," while the latter was dreaded by performers, insisting on the highest standards with numerous and exacting rehearsals. Certainly the film *Amadeus* vividly portrays Mozart's infectious enthusiasm on the podium.

THE CONDUCTOR AS INTERPRETER

With the expansion of the symphony and symphony orchestra in the latter half of the nineteenth century, the need for a conductor as an interpreter of the music as well as a time-beater became increasingly apparent. It became more difficult for players to be aware of the overall balance when performing as members of increasingly large orchestral and choral forces. Entries were less obvious in the musical score, dynamic variation increased, and more sensitive adjustment generally was needed to maintain a suitable balance and precision. Clearly the mechanisms by which a small classical orchestra could be kept together were unsuitable and insufficient for a Mahler or Bruckner symphony. The music of Berlioz and Wagner required an independent "specialist-conductor" with a baton, and both composers wrote treatises on this "new art."[4]

Carl Maria von Weber's influence on the development of conducting during the nineteenth century is outlined by Kreuger, who refers to him as "the first great master of modern conducting" who, as a broadly educated musician, "revealed a musical versatility which none of his contemporaries or forerunners possessed."[5] Weber is reputed to have rehearsed meticulously and imposed his artistic will on musicians in a friendly yet unyielding manner. Weber introduced the baton into the Dresden opera after successful experimentation in Prague, where it became the tool for ensuring homogeneous fusion of vocal and instrumental ensemble. A drawing by J. Hayter shows Weber conducting with a large baton in London in 1826.

Mendelssohn in 1835 provided direction and control over his music with a baton that put an end to the old method of violin direction at Leipzig; this meant that the Leipzig Gewandhaus Orchestra was one of the first to be regularly conducted. Some contemporary accounts (for example, Spohr's autobiography) suggest that the advent of the conductor brought orchestral playing to a higher degree of perfection. Accounts of Mendelssohn's relationship with the Gewandhaus reveal particular personality characteristics that must have had an important part to play in the development of the orchestra. A contemporary account, cited in Kreuger's book *The Way of the Conductor,* reveals that Mendelssohn's personality and interpersonal skills must have been significant in the development of the art of conducting:

> He approached his task with the devotion of a priest in the temple and, far from seeking to draw attention to himself, did everything to submerge himself in the orchestra. He even beat the second part of the triple bar to the left, where it was visible only to the orchestra! Contemporaries tell how the play of his expressive features mirrored the course of the music and how one could read the approaching nuances and effects on his mobile countenance.[6]

Berlioz, in his treatise on orchestration of 1855,[7] advocated the use of the baton and full orchestral score for the conductor. He was himself a fiery conductor and had an irresistible power of command when conducting his own music; however, accounts reveal him as lacking in the interpretation of other composers' works.[8] In addition, the writings of Wagner and Weingarten emphasized theories of the conductor's art and the emergence of a "true profession."[9]

The baton-conducting practice in the rest of Europe took several years to become established. In France it had a troubled development, with the practice of beating time audibly with a stick (as with Lully) still in evidence well into the nineteenth century notably in the Paris Opéra.[10] In Italy, the emergence of the baton-conductor was slower than in France, Germany, or England because the principal violinist was reluctant to relinquish his status. Using the violin bow as a means of conducting was clearly too cumbersome and inadequate to control large orchestral (and choral) forces. The violinist Habeneck (1781–1849) was likely to have been the last representative of the violinist-conductor of a large ensemble.

Spohr, writing in a letter to Wilhelm Speyer in 1820, described the customary practice of conducting in England as "topsy-turvey." Indeed, Spohr introduced the baton-conducting practice in opposition to the keyboard-director, and wrote of the result:

> The audience were at first startled by the novelty, and were seen whispering together; but when the music began and the orchestra executed the well-known symphony with unusual power and precision, the general approbation as shown immediately in the conclusion of the first part by a long-sustained clapping of hands. The triumph of the baton as a time giver was decisive, and no-one was seen anymore seated at the piano during the performances of symphonies and overtures.

Liszt supposedly was one of the first conductors to use gesture and facial expression to indicate the character of the music and to stamp a sense of individuality on a performance. Wagner also became a particularly expressive conductor, and his followers "who watched the rehearsals and performances conducted by this phenomenal artist whose glance beheld everything and whose facial expression and histrionic talents of communication were pronounced exceptional by the best actors, emerged as the first group of modern, thoroughly competent and devoted masters of the baton."[11]

However, it was a long time before the conductor's personality and individuality became a customary distinguishing feature of musical performances. Nineteenth-century audiences essentially came to hear the music, the virtuoso instrumentalist, and singer, not to see the conductor. It was only really in the twentieth century that conductors stamped their own interpretations distinctively on the orchestral repertoire. Some of the notable conductors were Arthur Nikisch (1855–1922), Arturo Toscanini (1867–1957), Willem Mengelberg (1871–1951), Fritz Reiner (1888–1963), Serge Koussevitsky (1874–1951), Wilhelm Furtwangler (1886–1954), and Bruno Walter (1876–1962). Each of these was noted for his distinctive style and idiosyncratic behaviors in rehearsal and performance, implanting particular interpretations on the music. It is not uncommon at the present time, and has been so throughout the twentieth century, for a conductor to receive as much notoriety as the composer or soloist in a performance. Evidence from personal experience acknowledges that the public flocked to see and hear, for example, the series of Beethoven symphonies conducted by Otto Klemperer in London shortly before his death in the early 1970s. Today such conductors as Zubin Mehta, Lorin Mazel, Michael Tilson Thomas, and Simon Rattle guarantee a large audience, as evidenced in the concert listings in the press.

THE CONDUCTOR OF CHORAL ENSEMBLES

Although today the conductor is regarded as an interpreter of music primarily in the orchestral field, choral groups have needed a person to "beat time" or control, in some way, the tempo of the music. In his book *The Great Conductors* Schoenberg charts the development of conducting from ancient times—"Horace asks the maidens and youths to pay attention to the Sapphic step and snap of his fingers. Thus Horace was, in a way, a conductor, marking the rhythms of his songs by foot and hand"—to the thirteenth century, when in *Tractus de Musica* by Elias Salomon, it is written that the conductor (one of the singers)

> has to know everything about the music to be sung. He beats time with his hand on the book and gives cues and rests to the singers. If one of them sings incorrectly, he whispers into his ear, "You are too loud, too soft, your tones are wrong," as the case may be, but so that the others do not hear it. Sometimes he must support them with his own voice if he sees that they are lost.[12]

The conductor was not really considered an interpreter of music until the nineteenth century, when large orchestral and choral forces and increasing demands of composers in terms of rubato phrasing, flexible tempi, and rhythmic complexity made the conductor a significant figure. Musical direction rather evolved from a need to control singers and instrumentalists. Evidence is provided, from bas reliefs and wall paintings in tombs dating from the ancient Sumerians c. 2270 B.C., the Egyptians c. 1400 B.C., and the ancient Greeks, as well as early Christian music, of some form of time beating or extrinsic hand gesture as being a notable feature of choral singing. Such art has provided some indication of musical practices from ancient history. Robinson and Winold suggest that there might have been some interpretative gesturing in Vedic music of India as well as in the rhythmically free chanting of early Christian music.[13] The presence of gestures in early cultures is noteworthy in that they point to conclusive evidence of the existence of some kind of central control in primitive choral performances.

Time beaters were in evidence in the Sistine Chapel Choir in the fifteenth century, where a roll of paper called a "sol-fa" was used to indicate the pulse of the music. Similar practices were in evidence in Elizabethan England and also in the time of Bach's predecessor at Leipzig. Some fourteenth- and sixteenth-century prints show groups of musicians and singers being led by a person with a stick or roll of paper. Morley, in his *Plaine and Easie Introduction to Practicall Musicke* of 1597, gives us the following:

PHILOMETHUS: What is a stroke?

MAGISTER: It is a successive motion of the hand, directing the quality of every note and rest in the song, with equal measure, according to the variety of signs and proportions.[14]

It is understandable that with rhythmically complicated, polyphonic music, some sort of control of the pulse and tempo would have been necessary. It is also evident that this was not so necessary in the seventeenth and eighteenth centuries, when choral music in England became less polyphonic and thus less complex rhythmically. During the early Baroque the emergence of the harpsichord and organ continuo enabled small groups of singers and instrumentalists to depend on the distinctive and percussive (in the case of the harpsichord) sound of such continuo instruments to keep the performances together and relatively unified in direction.

The performance venue would often dictate the need for a visual means of keeping time. This was the case in St. Mark's Venice, where large instrumental and choral forces were brought together, for example, in the antiphonal music of the Gabrielis and Monteverdi, in a vibrant acoustic space where groups of performers were often distant from each other. The music reflected and was written for the architecture of the building, the ground plan being in the shape of a spacious equilateral cross.

In 1737, the English composer William Boyce was appointed conductor of the Three Choirs Festival. Samuel Wesley (in a lecture given in 1827) reported that Boyce's method was "to mark out the measure to the orchestra with a roll of parchment or paper in his hand." It was also noted that Boyce "was a man of striking personality,"[15] which suggests that his appointment as conductor may have been influenced by this trait. He certainly adopted the method of conducting with a parchment and held his appointment at the Three Choirs Festival until deafness prevented him from continuing.

Following the deaths of Handel and Boyce, choral music, which had been strong since the Middle Ages in England, fell into decline, as a number of composers of inferior ability to Handel wrote oratorios and other choral pieces. However, during the latter part of the nineteenth century a revitalization of music generally and choral singing in particular took place. The work of John Curwen and Sarah Glover fostered interest in singing in schools and churches. Their prime concern was the improvement of sight-singing to enable church services to benefit. Such a profound effect did Curwen's tonic sol-fa scheme have on music education that great festivals of sight-singing took place in London's Crystal Palace and similar venues throughout the country often with 3,000 singers and audiences of some 30,000. Choral performances required a great degree of control by conductors because of their size, though the main objective was involvement of the masses in the singing of (usually) Handel oratorios.

The success of events like the Handel festivals, the first of which took place in 1784 in Westminster Abbey, stimulated the emergence of amateur choral societies in England and Germany, which developed throughout the nineteenth century. The two oratorios of Haydn, *The Creation* and *The Seasons,* exerted an influence on choral singing in Germany just as Handel's oratorios did in England. One of the first of such choirs, the Berlin Singakademie, gave a performance of Bach's *St. Matthew Passion,* conducted by Mendelssohn in 1829. Another significant choir was the Vienna Singverein, which in its early days was conducted by Brahms. Paralleling the rise in congregational hymn singing in Protestant churches and singing in schools, the amateur choral society flourished and extended its influence also to North America. One significant and pervading raison d'etre of these groups was to bring ordinary people into contact with choral literature, thus ennobling them through the cultivation of choral art.

The role of the choral conductor continued to develop in the latter half of the twentieth century. Choral compositions made increasing demands on the technical and interpretative skills of the conductor with, for example, increasingly complex rhythmic and harmonic structures as represented in the music of Britten, Bernstein, Tippett, and a generation of younger composers. The technological improvement of recording facilities has promoted smaller professional choirs performing to a very high standard. In conjunction, a revival of interest in Renaissance and early music has arisen, as well as a return, to simpler musical structures as represented in the music of minimalist composers such as Arvo Pärt and John Tavener.

PERSONALITY AND BEHAVIORAL CHARACTERISTICS OF CONDUCTORS

Historically, what most conductors have had in common is an acute ear, the charisma to inspire musicians

> on first acquaintance, the will to get their own way, high organizational ability, physical and mental fitness, relentless ambition, a powerful intelligence and a natural sense of order which enables them to cut through thousands of scattered notes to the artistic core.

So wrote Norman Lebrecht in the introduction to his book *The Maestro Myth*,[16] which attempts to expose some of the myths and mysteries surrounding the great conductors. Not only is this an investigation of the reasons for the successes of certain conductors, but it is also a rational treatise on the role played psychologically, socially, and musically by some of the most powerful (in the influential, musical sense) figures in recent Western musical civilization. The orchestral world has had many pioneering, domineering, and heroic figures as its conductors throughout the last 150 years or so. Furtwangler, Toscanini, Karajan, Klemperer, and Beecham, among many others, have cut a distinctive mold in this area; their names have often carried more weight (particularly in the areas of advertising and musical criticism) than the composers whose music they have interpreted. Tilson Thomas, Mehta, Barenboim, and Rattle are more recent examples of conductors who are sought after, not only by orchestras and their audiences, but also by recording companies, who see their names in terms of financial as well as musical prosperity. The character of the profession, insists Lebrecht, has been molded by the styles, personalities, and idiosyncratic behavior of powerful, Caucasian, and apparently heterosexual men (although with some notable exceptions):

> Taken from start to finish, the story of conducting is a chronicle of individual endeavour and ambition, modulated by violent circumstances in the surrounding society. Conducting, like most forms of heroism, rests on the use and abuse of power for personal benefit. Whether such heroism is desirable in music, or a necessary evil, remains open to debate.

Examples of the earlier conductors, from Hans von Bulow (1830–1894) onward, suggest that a conductor required some of the personality characteristics of a tyrannical dictator. Lebrecht points out that people such as Koussevitsky and Toscanini terrified their players by the manner in which they used their authority, often treating them like children in a very formal classroom. More contemporary comments of the characteristics and attributes of a successful conductor, which point to certain personality traits, are outlined by various established conductors including

Eugene Ormandy, who states: "He acts as a guide to the orchestra, building up in their minds a concept of the work parallel to his own, for the eventual public performance requires an enlightened and sensitive orchestra, playing not *under* a conductor, but rather *with* him."[17]

Adrian Boult was one of the few great conductors to write significantly about the conducting profession. In his small book *Thoughts on Conducting*, he states: "he must have a power of leadership, an infinite capacity for taking pains, unlimited patience and a real gift of psychology. He must have a constitution of iron and be ready to appear good-humoured in the face of the most maddening frustrations."[18]

It was Arthur Nikisch (1855–1922) who established much of the modern character of the conducting profession in his determination to make conducting a "creative" act rather than simply interpreting the composers' scores faithfully. He felt it important that each performance should have a degree of spontaneity and distinctiveness. Lebrecht notes, "Like love-making, Nikisch held that conducting required spontaneity, boldness, imagination and a profound feeling for the work in hand. Routine was abhorrent to him."[19] In addition, Nikisch was reputed to be popular with all orchestral players with whom he came into contact, and was generally affable and liberal in his praise toward them. He certainly became a model for a whole series of conductors who followed in the early twentieth century—Pierre Monteux, Ernest Ansermet, Fritz Reiner, Georg Szell, Eugene Ormandy, Georg Solti, and even Herbert von Karajan and Leonard Bernstein, to name a few. Adrian Boult admired Nikisch in particular for his effective stick technique and method of rehearsal, describing him as having a certain economy in his gesture:

> To begin with, he made his stick say more than any other conductor that I have ever watched. Its power of expression was so intense that one felt it would be quite impossible, for instance, to play *staccato* when Nikisch was showing a *legato*. There was no need for him to stop and ask for a *sostenuto*—his stick had already pulled it from the players.

Such evidence points to one of the key attributes of a conductor, namely the ability to extract the appropriate musical expression from the players and singers without excessive talk in rehearsals. Research also confirms that verbal explanations and verbal correcting of each inappropriate musical feature are not really necessary when acknowledgment and much effective correcting can be achieved by gesture and facial expression, particularly with highly trained professional orchestral players who already have a thorough grounding in the repertoire. The essence of the Nikisch style was to favor such an approach in rehearsal. (Nikisch also became one of the first conductors to command substantial financial reward for his work.) This is the case also with Bernard Haitink, who, in a recent radio program celebrating his musical directorship of the Royal Opera House, Covent Garden in London, was praised by a number of orchestral players for his efficient and non-verbal rehearsal style.

Lebrecht, through detailed qualitative research, makes remarks on the personalities of many conductors. He describes the tenacious character of Karajan, a personality and figure of power admired by Helmut Schmidt (sometime West German chancellor) and Margaret Thatcher (sometime British prime minister). Not only have we here a conductor of some reputation, but also a person whose "personal relations were, like all his prodigious gifts and possessions, permanently at the service of a higher cause—the pursuit of total and eternal power." Karajan himself was concerned to find out some of the psychological and psychobiological effects and stresses that music had on conductors as well as listeners. He founded a Research Institute for Experimental Psychology at the University of Salzburg, where he took part in experiments monitoring pulse rates, blood pressure, and static electricity on his skin. He believed in a "whole body" approach to conducting, which enabled him to keep youthful. He learned to breathe freely during tense moments in the music and was a yoga fanatic. Helen Matheopoulos, in her book *Maestro*, which describes encounters with conductors from personal interviews, wrote, in relation to Karajan, that the mystery of the art of conducting "cannot be explained in concrete terms... [sic] like the healing effect of music both on those who listen and on those who make it and are constantly renewed by the hidden force inherent in and emanating from it."[20]

Bernstein, who suggested in an interview with Matheopoulos that it is "the most potent love affair you can have in your life," acknowledges the mystery of conducting. The flamboyant composer-player-conductor reduced the art of conducting to love. "We love one another. Every orchestra I conduct is a love affair" (ibid., 11).

Bernstein here goes beyond the notion of "loving" the music as enjoying or simply liking it, but rather draws a deeper analogy of people coming together to discover new music and fulfilling a musical need with sexual satisfaction. He also draws a compelling comparison between conducting and the process of composing: "I'm composing the piece as we go along: now, I bring in F sharp, now we bring in the basses, next the trombones, now we bring in the choir. It's an unbelievable experience, as if I were composing a piece which I knew very well on the spot" (ibid., 12).

Such a creative approach to the art of conducting supports the notion that something new and spontaneous is needed in each musical performance, not only for the listeners in the audience, but also for the performers, to enrich the musical event in a meaningful way. Bernstein has indeed been noted, by various critics, for his "extreme" interpretations and extravagant gestures, but his performances have undoubtedly also created reactions, which players and singers who have worked with him have recognized. One notable controversy was his intention in 1977 to conduct a performance of Beethoven's C sharp minor quartet, Opus 131 with the full strings of the Vienna Philharmonic Orchestra. His powers of persuasion and personality made it work, and, after much disagreement Bernstein started: "after half an hour of the first rehearsal, there were tears in their eyes" (ibid., 17). One measurement of an effective conductor can be evaluated by the reception and reaction of orchestral players and singers, who are notoriously skeptical of a new person on the podium. This account points to the fact that Bernstein was obviously successful in his dealings with the Vienna Philharmonic and was generally able to capture the admiration of many under him.

Although he never really came to like conducting and maintained a love-hate relationship with it, Benjamin Britten regularly conducted his own and other people's music during most of his active working life. Many players and singers have found his conducting inspiring. Humphrey Carpenter, in his biography of Britten, quoted several. Emanuel Hurvitz, sometime leader of the Glyndebourne and English Chamber Orchestras, said: "Players would give just anything for Ben to be conducting rather than anyone else. . . . He was a conductor who made the orchestra feel they wanted to play for him."[21]

The harpist Osian Ellis points out that Britten knew the names of his players and liked them, thus perhaps accounting for him as "the one conductor who made you play your best—you couldn't do enough for him. I don't know another conductor who does that for you" (ibid., 251). Much of Britten's own music was choral and vocal, and my own experiences of singing in a choir with him conducting certainly validate these comments. Acute musical sensitivity and understanding were some of the conducting attributes that he conveyed to the performers (and audience). His conducting has inspired many professional singers. One notable example is Janet Baker, who referred to "his marvellous shaping of the phrase but at the same time [one was] given room, a sort of freedom, to yield to the inspiration of the moment. Only the very greatest conductors have this ability" (ibid.).

A great deal of the anecdotal evidence describing impressions that particular conductors have made on performers and audiences is curiously nebulous in attempting to define, with any specificity, an effective conductor. All the features of character and personality mentioned in these anecdotes give some indications of what makes an effective conductor, but it is apparent that all such characteristics do not match all good conductors. For some, stick technique is considered important; while Nikisch had it, Britten, according to himself and others, did not. Boulez does not use one. Yet each, in his own individual style is, or has been, considered an effective or even "great" conductor.

Boult prepared a formidable (by contemporary norms) list of qualifications for the practicing conductor, which, if taken literally, would ensure that very few today would actually aspire to such musical heights. (It suggests, for example that an orchestral conductor should be a proficient player on five instruments.) Most of the writing in his book is concerned with the technical aspects of conducting taken from a personal standpoint; its tenor is much like an advice manual, suggesting what to do and what not to do. Boult does, however, make an analogy between rehearsing and teaching, saying that the role of the conductor in this context is to stimulate and motivate the musician to listen, think, and react to what is going on around him. He suggests, for example, that the use of positive comments during rehearsals are much more helpful in creating a pleasant working environment and good personal relationships than are negative comments such as "Don't . . . !" Here he promotes the idea of rehearsing to get the feel of the whole piece rather than perfecting bar by bar, which he associates with an atomistic and what he refers to as an "American" approach. Nevertheless, his principles accord with the human-compatible learning concept outlined in chapter 2; it's about getting the best out of people. The only real reference Boult makes to working with amateur choirs, from his own experience as conductor of the Bach Choir, is to propose a plan of the rehearsals that should be followed. Boult's own perception of the role of the conductor was more in line with the "chairman of the committee," which often made him appear efficient but somewhat dull in comparison with some of his contemporaries such as Beecham or Sargent. However, Norman Lebrecht suggests that Boult was a musician of exceptional sensitivity and intelligence, qualities that he hid behind the stiff British bristle that decorated his upper lip.

Looking at the role of the orchestral and choral conductor in their historical contexts has suggested that increasingly personality and behavioral traits have shaped the art of conducting into what it has become today. It is apparent that much of what has counted as effective conducting, or what has made a conductor "great," has been partly dependent on personality and the ability to inspire. Various conductors appear dependent on a sense of authority that enables them to get what they want from players and singers; some are reputedly tyrannical, some gentle.

Yet, those they conduct have seen them all as superb musicians. In discussion with a retired horn player from one famous American orchestra, I discovered that even players who were verbally abused by particular conductors were nevertheless inspired by their musicianship. Certain sets of musical skills, particularly aural ones, clearly must be in place. In addition, certain characteristics seem important judging from several biographical sources. Awareness of the aesthetic and expressive potential of music, sensitivity, and a wide musical knowledge are desirable prerequisites. Also, most of the renowned conductors are able to articulate a philosophy on which they base their conducting technique and interpretations of music. These descriptive and anecdotal accounts differ as to whether conductors need to be trained or already have the essential musical and technical skills in place. The different messages outlined in this section have highlighted the complexity of the nature of human communication and interaction as well as the conducting phenomenon itself. As with other areas of musical interaction, there are plenty of issues to consider.

So what can we learn from the great conductors and the past? This book is certainly not intended for the great conductors of professional orchestras. Yet they seem to be the ones who have had the most attention. There may be things that we can cull from the information about them that will be relevant for the conductor of an elementary school choir or a rural community chorus. As I have already pointed out, it is important to be respected musically by those you conduct, and your interpersonal skills need not be the dictatorial or tyrannical aspects associated with some of the "greats." So to whom are we referring? Where does the conducting happen and whom does it happen for?

CATEGORIES OF CHORAL CONDUCTING

Choral conducting is an activity that exists extensively in Western culture. It has been practiced over centuries, and there is no real evidence to show that the activity itself is less prevalent now than in the past. In

PROFESSIONAL	COMMUNITY	SCHOOL	CHURCH
Specialist choirs	Choral societies	Primary/elementary	Cathedral/church
Symphony choruses	Barber shop	High & junior high/ secondary/specialist	College & community chapel
Cathedral/church choirs	Small informal groups	University/college	Small local church setting

order to provide some sort of operational definition for the purposes of this book, it might be interesting to outline the categories of choral conducting activity and their parameters. Put simply, a lot of people do it, at a variety of musical and educational levels. The categories identified are not intended to be hierarchical or exhaustive in any way.

"Professional" is a term used to denote those who are paid for their service. Nowadays, the conductors of professional choirs, including small chamber groups sometimes specializing in the performance of Renaissance or contemporary music, for example, fall into this category. A number of cathedral and collegiate chapel choirs in North America as well as in Europe make recordings of music intended for the liturgy.

Conducting a youth choir.

Conducting a rehearsal of a choir and orchestra in St. Alban's Cathedral, England.

Some of these conductors and their choirs gain their reputation through their recordings and concert tours around the world and are acknowledged experts in a particular specialist field. The "star" conductors of the world's major orchestras also have in their repertoire a large number of major choral works that they perform in concert halls around the world.

Choral works such as the requiems of Verdi and Berlioz and the second and eighth symphonies of Mahler require very large forces and can be performed only in suitably large venues. The chorus master, who will have the responsibility for training large symphonic choirs, may well not conduct the actual performances.

A more extensive group of choral conductors work with choral societies and similar community choirs. They conduct amateur and local groups, perhaps reflecting the town, city, or area in their name. In North America they became known also as choral societies, musical associations, or even singing clubs. One noted choral society was in Stoughton, Massachusetts, and evolved from William Billings's singing school in 1774. According to Michael Mark and Charles Gary there were more than a hundred choral societies in Massachusetts between 1785 and 1840; all were concerned with the promotion of sacred music. Immigrants from Europe, in particular from Germany, where choral singing was prominent at the beginning of the nineteenth century, helped to ensure the continuation of these choirs.[22]

These groups helped spread the idea that ordinary people could be led into special experiences within their communities by the "ennobling" cultivation of choral art. The idea that "workers" could be brought out of their common existence through experiences of high art became widespread in Europe, in, for example, areas like the mining communities of South Wales with their famous Welsh male voice choirs. The use of the word "ennoble" by many contemporary writers indicates the ways in which it was believed that choral music had the potential to elevate people in taste and status (and also the somewhat demeaning view that these writers had of common people). Such development heralded an increase in output of new choral pieces for large and smaller choirs and glee clubs. Charles Villiers Stanford, Hubert Parry, and Arthur Sullivan were among the prominent composers who led the Renaissance in England; their large- and small-scale choral works represent the most significant part of their output. As they abandoned the traditional recitative-aria-chorus oratorio structure and opted for a more Wagnerian influenced "romantic" style of composing, there was a necessity for the conductor to do more than keep time. Elgar's *Dream of Gerontius* is one example of an oratorio that abandons set arias and recitatives, adopting a through-composed seamless structure. This work demands a knowledgeable conductor to be properly sung; in fact, its premiere in Birmingham in 1900 was not performed well at all, with the choir inadequately prepared. This performance also shook the choral community and established the conductor as a distinctive interpreter of the music as well as controller of the performers. (My own experience tells me that *Dream of Gerontius* offers a significant but worthwhile challenge to the conductor.)

Consequently, a new generation of choral conductors emerged taking the role of controller and interpreter of large forces singing the standard oratorio repertoire. The tradition of choral societies continued with the performances of oratorios by Handel, Haydn, Mendelssohn, and the newer composers, including Elgar and Vaughan Williams, who were prominent in the early part of the twentieth century. The conductor was featured in both amateur and professional capacities, but the role was essentially the same. The conductor was needed to provide the mechanisms for keeping large forces together as well as to create a single, unified expressive interpretation of the music.

Another significant area of growth at the beginning of the twentieth century was in patriotic and nationalist songs. This occurred in countries in Europe and also in North America, coinciding with the outbreak of the First World War. These songs were sung in community situations including schools and stirred feelings of patriotism in each country. Such songs were also sung in the military to preserve morale.

Most British towns and cities, for example, still boast community choirs or something similar. This is also the case in a number of European countries, notably in Scandinavia and Germany, also increasingly in Estonia and Latvia. These choirs vary in size, quality, and experience and are likely to be of amateur status. Concerts performed locally may involve professional orchestras and professional singers as soloists, but the conductor in the performance will normally be the conductor who trains and rehearses the choir. Repertoires range from large-scale oratorios, such as *Messiah* and *Elijah,* to smaller sacred and secular choral works of a wide selection of composers.

Many choral conductors work in schools. Singing is positively promoted as a performing activity within the school music curriculum of many countries, including England and Wales. A large proportion of schools both in the primary and secondary sectors in the United Kingdom, for example, have choral singing as an extracurricular activity in addition to its place in the general classroom. The situation in North America is probably more stable, with choirs often being an integral part of the school day for many students. Choral singing in schools in North America grew steadily during the late nineteenth and early twentieth centuries with, for example, the Pennsylvania Secondary Schools Classification Directory in 1928 requiring one period a week of "general chorus" throughout the school year. There is evidence of the popularity of the major oratorios of Handel and Haydn being performed by some school choirs.[23] In the 1930s in American high schools, a cappella singing became increasingly common, setting the standards for some high-quality choral achievements during that decade. With the onset of radio broadcasting and the rise of instrumental programs in schools, choral directors were stimulated into creating and maintaining high-level choral programs. Also, the music contests and festivals continue to be a particular American tradition, organized countywide, statewide, and nationally. This has enabled some choral directors and their choirs to gain status within the schools and the community.

Today in North America a number of school conductors have daily contact with their choirs—less common an occurrence perhaps in European schools. It is nevertheless to be expected that each choir will have a choral conductor or director who may lead the singing from an instrument—the guitar or piano, for example. Some teachers do not easily think of themselves as conductors or choral directors and are often apologetic about their efforts in this field. One of my graduate students—a choral director working in a challenging middle school in the Washington, D.C. area—was somewhat apologetic concerning his choral conducting skills. He maintained that his real expertise was as a pianist and therefore tended to direct from the piano rather than stand confidently in front of his choir classes.

Choral activities in schools as with other amateur choirs will range in quality and experience. As adjudicator of school choral festivals in the United States, I have witnessed the range, but have also been impressed by the high standards of choral singing achieved by some choirs. Conductors are often music teachers who spend the majority of time on general class music. In the case of primary or elementary school teachers, they may teach other, non-music subjects, and the choirs are likely to operate in extracurricular time, or, as in some European countries, in specialist conservatories in the community. Some primary or elementary schools that have no music specialist may employ a choral conductor or recruit a volunteer to rehearse and perform with a choir. The repertoire is wide-ranging and dependent on the interests of the conductor and students, but generally includes standard choral repertoire and music from jazz and popular idioms as well as non-Western styles.

There are widespread concerns regarding the recruitment of boys in particular to school choirs and with regard to singing activity in adolescence in general.[24] This appears to be the case universally and may well be to do with vocal maturational concerns as well as repertoire and sociocultural issues. (I will address some aspects regarding the conductor and adolescent singers in chapter 9.) Nevertheless, there are pockets of fine choral practice in schools around the world. The range of quality in school choirs begs the question as to whether effective conducting is a product of training, innate musical ability, or the natural infectious enthusiasm of a teacher who would inspire in any subject.

A fourth area of choral activity is in the churches, cathedrals, and college chapels around the world. These have established the foundation on which the choral reputation of the country lies, as in the case of England. People around the world associate choral singing in England with boys' choirs and cathedrals. Most British cathedrals maintain regular (in some cases daily) singing of the services. This is a significant choral tradition, though involving a relatively small number of highly selected singers. A cathedral choir will typically have as few as twelve boy sopranos and two each of altos (male), tenors, and basses. A cathedral choir of 32 or more is considered large, as will be found in the larger cathedrals like St. Paul's in London. Apart from in the cathedrals, male only choirs are less prevalent today than previously, and it has become common for church choirs to be of mixed gender as in other countries such as Sweden and the United States, for example. There are examples of excellent church choirs throughout each country that continue to exist for a variety of reasons. In each there will be a conductor, or more usually in most of Europe, an organist, who will assume responsibility for the choir, and perhaps lead the singing from the organ or actually conduct if there is an assistant organist or the music is unaccompanied.

The significance of singing, both in choral settings of the liturgy (the sections of the Mass, for example) and to enhance worship through hymn singing or to create a particular mood, is paramount. Although music for the church has suffered from rather ordinary and often uninspired compositions, not just today but throughout the ages, and particularly in the nineteenth century, there are, nevertheless, a great number of musical gems that have captured the imaginations of conductors and singers.

These categories indicate the formal side of choral conducting and the public awareness of this activity. Of course, choral conducting also occurs in a variety of informal, even casual, situations. In some of these occasions someone may be conducting, which might simply involve indicating the tempo for the start of the music, for example, when a group is singing Christmas carols to collect money for charity outside a supermarket. Thus, a significant number and variety of people are involved in choral conducting or directing of some sort, so effectiveness needs to be considered and evaluated in relation to the context in which it occurs. As with teaching and other professions, so choral conducting has a range of recognizable skills, which are evaluated continually by those being conducted, those listening to the performances, and even the conductors themselves. The expectations of those listening will vary according to the context; the criteria for evaluating a performance of a professional chamber choir will be different from those of a performance of a primary or elementary school choir, as the expectations from the conductor and audience will be different.

So, maybe there are common criteria used by singers and listeners when judging and evaluating conductors. Singers presumably compare conductors, asking themselves what makes one conductor more effective than another. An interesting question is whether a successful conductor in one context would be successful in another. How would Ricardo Muti do in front of a middle school choir? Does one particular category of choral conducting demand its own specific competence? Or are there generic competences for all categories of choral conductors? There are clearly aspects of conducting that relate to personality characteristics; can any characteristics be identified that are common to all choral conductors? Are effective conductors born or made?

In a series of auditions for conducting students, I reflected on some of these questions. Over a period of weeks, a number of university choir rehearsals were given over to budding graduates who came to audition for admission by taking part of the rehearsal. Some candidates were clearly more at ease than others; some had a secure conducting technique, while others clearly had less developed skills. Some of these conductors also communicated their understanding of the music and attended to vocal issues; others did not. In summing up and inevitably comparing one with another, I began to consider not just their technical conducting competence and musical and vocal knowledge, but also their interpersonal skills. Who really communicated their enthusiasm for the music and engaged the student choir? One student, for example, ran a slick, competent, but dull rehearsal; she clearly had musical ability and knowledge. Another showed less secure conducting technique but engaged the singers more. In evaluating these two candidates, the next question to consider was: Which aspect of conducting is teachable? Can conducting technique be taught? I hope so. Can communication and interpersonal skills be taught? I would like to think so, but I am not 100 percent sure. Which candidate would benefit from the graduate position most? Which one had the potential to be superb? With whom can teachers of conducting make most difference?

The areas addressed so far raise more questions than they answer. I shall attempt to explore the whole issue of human interactions at the center of the conducting activity. I want to link the more scientific approach to human behavior and learning, as outlined in chapter 2, with the conducting phenomenon itself, explaining what we as conductors do to bring out the best in those we conduct. We already have some examples illustrating people's positive responses to particular conductors. If singing is so integral to humanity, let us explore what conductors are doing to preserve our humanity, to make sense of our world and our music.

5

THE CHORAL CONDUCTING
PHENOMENON

In order to identify some of the characteristics of effective choral conducting, let's look at the nature and intricacy of conducting and the
contexts within which such activity occurs. We will look behind the
phenomenon at the kinds of conducting skill and knowledge that will
help us better define what makes for good choral conducting. We will
explore the phenomenon itself, and, in terms of teaching and learning in the choral rehearsal, the associated types of craft and knowledge
that support human-compatible learning and communication. The term
"human compatible" already suggests a style of communication, one of
careful and thoughtful interaction that enables people to feel positive
about a musical learning experience. Through such exploration we will
consider many of the attributes, skills, and strategies desirable for effective choral conducting, and, consequently, a clearer conception of what
in conducting is teachable (and learnable) might emerge. We are hop-
ing to define "human-compatible conducting," if you like. We may well
then become more informed and able to design conducting courses and
workshops as well as learn more about our own conducting.

PHENOMENOLOGY AND CONDUCTING

Phenomenology essentially refers to what the philosopher Husserl describes as "the things themselves";[1] in other words, the actual events that
we experience and the impact that they have on us. Much of our examination and exploration of conducting will focus on descriptions of what

people do when they conduct and the experiences they create for those they conduct.

Because I intend to present a philosophy of choral conducting, some exploration of philosophical inquiry is desirable. Can we answer all our questions about the nature of good choral conducting by engaging in experimental research? I already prefer to think not; at least we will not get the full picture. In describing methods of philosophical inquiry within music education, Phelps, Ferrara, and Goolsby refer to the philosopher Heidegger's view that "all knowledge gathered by traditional research methods in the natural and human sciences is ultimately circular. Verification or corroboration of results takes place within the confines of the theory that structures the research project."[2] They suggest that experimental research does not adequately inform us of the nature of the relationship and rapport between people: teachers and their students or conductors and their choirs. As in essence this part of the book is philosophical, it is unwise to expect that any research fieldwork or experimental design will conclusively inform us about the nature of effective choral conducting. That is not, however, to say that observation of practice or other research tools are not relevant or important. Nevertheless, the nature of effectiveness in choral conducting can only fully be understood in relation to the context in which the choral conducting operates. What conductors do that makes them successful at conducting in one context may not be valid and appropriate in another.

Some questions:

- Is it possible that unidentified elements will have applicability and validity for all types of conductors?
- Can the mystique of the conductor have the same effect with a school choir as it may have, say, in a large symphony chorus or a professional chamber choir?
- How does a conductor know how to behave or react in differing contexts?

Heidegger's approach to aesthetic inquiry (an interpretive phenomenological one) describes art as "dynamic happening"; it is interaction that makes it dynamic. He makes the distinction between "earth" *(erde)* and "world" *(welt)* as two of the fundamental elements of works of art. Earth is concerned with the materials of art: the sound in music, as paint in painting or stone in sculpture. These materials are clearly essential to art; the Greek temple cannot exist without the stone. However, Heidegger adds another level—the world—being concerned with contextualization, and it is this that gives art meaning. The formation of a beautiful Greek temple with stone within its religious and artistic context stimulates our appreciation of it, in contrast to the stones that lie on the path, or the stone slab that forms a bench to sit on, which are functional. The aesthetic element of the artwork can be understood only in terms of its context.

With reference to conductors and their choirs, the implication is that we can respond to the aesthetic and expressive potential in the performance or rehearsal only by acknowledging the context in which the art (in this case, the singing) occurs. The sound itself will not suffice; rather, we are dependent on the expressive potential of the music and the conductors' interpretations and conveyance of that potential, be it a simple reflective Christmas carol sung by small children, or a rousing *Hallelujah* chorus performed by a large choir in a vast cathedral. A phenomenological approach to choral conducting is then concerned with the dynamic interaction or "happening" between conductor and singers.

We should be encouraged as researchers in the arts to consider the artistic, the mystical, and the dynamics of interactions and happenings. As Phelps and his colleagues note:

> The strife between the earth and the world is possible only if an appreciating person allows that strife to show itself. Moreover, researchers must allow themselves to be transported into the world of the artist.... This definition of art as a dynamic happening signals the need for an eclectic method that is responsive to the multidimensional thrust that music is capable of providing.[3]

We need to take a refreshing, phenomenological, holistic approach in our research to help us unveil the magic and mystique of musical encounter and discover what makes it happen. If it is dynamic happening that matters in the creation of a work of art, then we should look at the whole picture, the whole phenomenon, and draw analysis in terms of what we see, hear, and feel, in preference to what we can count. In other words, let us research these questions *qualitatively*. We are dealing with people interacting with people and creating an artistic human phenomenon: music.

KNOWING-IN-ACTION AND TACIT KNOWING

Before the interaction can take place, conductors must know instinctively that they have an ability to lead people in certain musical actions, whether it is with a small elementary school choir or a large symphony chorus. Some conductors and teachers simply say they know that they can conduct or teach. Interviewing a prospective undergraduate student for admission to a music education program recently, I asked why he thought he could teach. He replied briskly and persuasively and with his eyes wide open, "I *know* I can." I was convinced by his answer.

Comparisons might be made with other fields of activity. Is becoming a tennis player, for example, something that is worked at, and is there an additional personal knowing that such achievements are possible? Has everyone the potential capability to become a tennis player or choral conductor, a photographer or a plumber? While clearly environmental factors will play a large part in influencing outcomes, what part does a tacit knowing play in the evolution of such skills in particular people?

The concept of "knowing-in-action" is discussed by Donald Schon, who refers to it as the type of knowledge or know-how in which our knowledge is revealed through intelligent *action:* "We reveal it by our spontaneous, skillful execution of the performance; and we are characteristically unable to make it verbally explicit."[4] This is the fundamental nature of success in any form of music making—its often "verbal inexplicitness."

Conductors, as anecdotal reference will bear out, are not always able to account for their actions or reason for their success, and often prefer to allude to the mystery of conducting. However, Schon suggests that it is possible, by reflecting on actions, to describe the tacit knowing implicit in them. Conductors will, on reflection, be able to articulate and rationalize why certain rehearsals go particularly well. I am also sure that most conductors and teachers can recall a particular collective emotional or meaningful aesthetic moment in a rehearsal or performance. There was one particular rehearsal with my community choir of Poulenc's *Gloria* that immediately comes to my mind. It was the end of a long and productive rehearsal nearing the performance date; the last movement rests on a sensuous and quiet ending undulating extensively on a sumptuous major 7th chord, which follows an energetic opening section. Somehow, all the conditions were in place for a communal recognition of something beautiful happening. I didn't have to say anything at the end—in fact I was unable to. It was also one of my last rehearsals with them for a year. The specific rehearsal conditions, the choir members' technical and vocal skills that were improving, the music itself as the catalyst, and the fact that I was leaving the choir for a while to spend some time in the United States all contributed to the special moment. There was a *connection* here, and the nature of the connection was dynamic: the dynamic interaction enabling special moments to occur. We should all remember those special moments, as they are the key to why we do what we do. This perhaps represents the essence of the conducting phenomenon.

Reference to the "sequences of operations and procedures, the clues and rules we follow, the values, strategies and assumptions that make up our 'theories' of action," as Schon suggests, can enable clearer under-standing of the type of knowing that is often not verbalized. This is the type of knowing that is implicit in the seemingly spontaneous actions of the conductor. Schon states that knowing-in-action is dynamic, in con-trast to "facts," "procedures," "rules," and "theories," which are static. What make the actions of the conductor intelligent are the continu-ous quick decision making, the detection and correction of errors, and adjustments that are the characteristic features of efficient rehearsals and even the performance. Anticipation of problems, gained through intimate knowledge of the score related to knowledge of the singers' capabilities, is part of the skill of the conductor in a rehearsal or per-formance. The adjustments in response to variations in the phenomena can be carried out by the "deployment of wide-ranging images of con-texts and actions" gained from conductors' previous experiences and knowledge. Knowing when, for example, to concentrate on a particu-lar technical detail of a small musical passage in a rehearsal or when to go for a more holistic feeling of the whole piece is an example of a knowing-in-action moment that enables a conductor to respond to the needs of the choir there and then.

The concept of "tacit knowing" is articulated by Michael Polanyi,[5] who refers to "knowing more than we can tell" and also, in relation to art, "indwelling"—entering into a work of art—as a way of understanding meaning. Understanding the phenomenon of conducting can be fully established only by being a part of the conducting phenomenon. Polanyi points out that indwelling as part of the structure of tacit knowing enables us to uncover meanings rather than just describe observations. He goes on to argue that scrutiny of particulars of a comprehensive entity often destroys our conception of the whole. We can take the point further in relation to our understanding of musical concepts. Our understanding of the aesthetic and expressive potential of a piece of music, and the effectiveness of a conductor in relation to it, accordingly, is more likely to materialize by "dwelling in" the entity than by making close analysis of the constituent elements: that is the phenomenological approach. My own belief is that a more effective approach to conducting is to first attend to the whole musical experience, by concentrating on the whole expressive intention of music. We should beware of ignoring the expressive elements during our rehearsals and concentrating on the technical. Somehow we need to allow our singers to dwell in the music, to understand something of its expressive character.

In the context of a learning situation, Harry Broudy presents Polanyi's distinctions between *focal* knowing (i.e., knowing something specific) and *tacit* knowing, explaining that the arts, as moral education for example, call upon a variety of approaches and modes of response to facilitate understanding. He distinguishes aesthetic learning as requiring perception accompanied by "imaginative reconstruction," as "all aesthetic expression is indirect and metaphorical."[6] We do not construct literal meaning in creating artistic forms, certainly not with music: as the most abstract of art forms, how can we? Experience of actual conducting, of being conducted and by listening to the outcomes—the *indwelling* in the entity (Broudy's "knowing with")—can provide us with insight into the nature and definition of what makes the phenomenon effective. That is why my text is peppered with examples of real conducting and singing situations that I have witnessed: it is the indwelling that informs.

CRAFT KNOWLEDGE

Throughout this book I use the term "craft" extensively with reference to conducting and teaching skills. Indeed, I emphasize the correlation between conducting and teaching, because I believe conducting, certainly in the rehearsal context, is essentially teaching. Conducting is often, and teaching is occasionally, referred to as an "art." However, Brown and McIntyre put forward the notion of teaching as "craft" knowledge and seek, through their own research, to identify definitions or states of effectiveness in teaching generally. Not wishing to denigrate the teaching profession by the implication that it is *just* a craft, Brown and McIntyre clarify that craft knowledge is part of the practical experience of the teacher. It is "integrated into the totality of their professional knowledge with all its broader educational and political features." As with my intention in this book with regard to choral conducting, so Brown and McIntyre confirm:

> Our concern is limited to the study and the articulation of the relatively routine and familiar aspects of what teachers do in classrooms, and with how they do the things they regularly do well. We are seeking knowledge which is potentially generalizable (and so can be shared) and the notion of professional *craft* knowledge is the best metaphor we can think of. Teachers' flashes of artistic genius will be a bonus.[7]

The comparison bears consideration; while there will be recognizable flashes of artistic genius in the conductors' work, day-to-day rehearsal situations may primarily draw on conductors' craft knowledge—the relatively routine and familiar aspects of what conductors do well.

A philosophical approach to the notion of *craft* in relation to *art* was articulated in 1938 by Collingwood, who, in developing a theory of art, referred to technique as an essential tool of the craftsman; however, he maintained that technique is insufficient in itself to make the craftsman an artist. To illustrate this he makes an enlightening reference to *Hymn* by the sixteenth-century English poet Ben Jonson. He states that while Jonson had the skills of "ingenious patterns of rhythm and rhyme, alliteration, assonance and dissonance" displayed in the poem, it was "his imaginative vision of the goddess and her attendants, for whose expression it was worth his while to use that skill."[8] We can certainly appreciate this example with Jonson's lines: "Hesperus entreats thy light/Goddess excellently bright." We can also attest to the artistry and craftsmanship of Benjamin Britten, who composed a most imaginative setting of this poem in his *Serenade for Tenor, Horn and Strings*. Artists need skill, and will more likely produce greater works of artistic merit with better technique, because they will be more able to illustrate their artistic imagery and insights. However, artists are dependent on imaginative vision, which was clearly in evidence in both Jonson's poem and Britten's setting of it.

Skilled craftsmen, suggested Collingwood, use knowledge as the means necessary to realize a given end, and it is the mastery of these means that is the craftsmen's skill. Using an example of a joiner making a table, Collingwood pointed out that he has at his disposal knowledge of materials and tools that are required to produce the specified table. So, ideally, teachers and choral conductors have equivalent knowledge to be able to realize their specified goals. In the rehearsal situation, conductors will call upon a repertoire of means to attain the performance goal, and it is their mastery of the various technical skills, understanding of what is required in order to achieve goals, which will make them craftsmen in rehearsal.

Yet the question remains, do conductors need that imaginative vision in a rehearsal situation or is it something only for the conductor in performance? If conductors have aesthetic sensitivity (surely the quality that is required to distinguish the artist from the craftsman), this must surely be displayed in rehearsal as well as in performance in order that the choir becomes immersed in the expressive potential of the music. That imaginative vision will need preparation and, consequently, the technique of rehearsing must seek for and encourage a sequence of appropriate responses from the singers. So, while conductors will have the craft knowledge and will know how to proceed in order to attain technical goals, they will also have the vision to guide the rehearsing toward the aesthetic goals.

Another educationalist, F. Elbaz, studied teachers' craft knowledge and identified five "orientations of practical knowledge":

(i) *situational* orientation, which is formulated according to the classroom, the school, the curriculum, and so forth
(ii) *personal* orientation, in which the teacher's knowledge

encompasses not only intellectual belief, but also perception, feeling, values, and commitment

(iii) *social* orientation, which is shaped by social constraints and is used to structure the social reality of the knower

(iv) *experiential* orientation, in which practical knowledge is shaped by multi-dimensional experiences

(v) *theoretical* orientation, which determines the contours of practical knowledge by the teacher's considered relationship between theory and practice.[9]

These categories clearly can also be applied to the choral rehearsal.

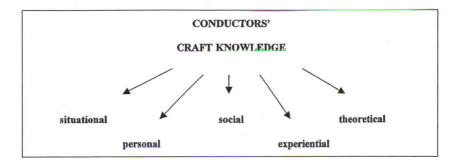

First, conductors' craft knowledge is modified by the *situation,* the size and composition of the choir, the setting, the repertoire, the overall context in which the choir operates—all of which constitute a type of knowing that is, or becomes, instinctive to the conductor. This is the type of knowing that will enable conductors to contextualize the approach they take with different choral groups. On a more technical level, for example, it will enable conductors to know how to deal with specific acoustics in the rehearsal room, which may influence the singers' intonation, balance, and blend.

Second, the conductors' craft knowledge is shaped by their *personal* philosophy (the principles underlying knowledge and actions) and commitment as well as the personal perception, reaction, and response presented during the rehearsal period. Third, the *social* dimension of the conductor's craft knowledge will be influenced by the nature of the group being conducted. This in turn will have a bearing on the choice and appropriateness of repertoire for the particular group and the conductors' expectations in respect of the learning rate, motivational factors, and general progression of the choir. This commits conductors to developing effective communication skills in addition to understanding various social factors concerning the choral group.

Fourth, the *experiential* base of teachers' and conductors' knowledge will impact on all of these decisions, because it is experience that shapes, influences, and alters the actions that people make. It is the phenomenology of conducting that is implicit in actions, allied to the tacit knowing that certain things we do promote certain outcomes. Experience tells conductors that a particular gesture will inform the choir of the particular sound they need to make in keeping with the character of the music; the anticipated response will be brought about with or without verbal prompting.

Finally, the *theoretical* aspects of the conductors' worlds are formed not only by their academic and musical training, but also by general discourse and choral and conducting developments of the day. This might include, for example, reflecting on new releases of choral works on CD, video and television close-ups of conductors in action in rehearsal and performance, as well as reading relevant journals and articles. In a sense, the professional development of conductors is a vital area that can stimulate and innovate in what could otherwise become an isolated and stale environment. Conductors tend not to work directly with other conductors, which makes conventions, meetings, and educational courses all the more important to maintain interest and creativity, be it by providing new repertoire, new warm-up ideas, or even an awakening from bad conducting habits. Let's not be defensive about our conducting; rather we should engage in real professional discourse and development.

The craft of conducting then is involved with the everyday normal rehearsal, where careful progression in the standard of achievement in the performance of the piece of music is an essential part of the conductors' responsibility. This progress will be maintained and directed by the ability of conductors to interest and motivate their singers in a human-compatible way. In the same way that teachers in the classrooms need strategies for motivating pupils, so the conductors need a different set of strategies for maintaining singers' motivation and progress, which will differ according to the social, professional, and musical context. As explained in chapter 2, teachers and conductors will ideally know something about the way people learn (yes, even to the extent of gaining a glimmer of insight into the neuropsychobiological sciences). At the rehearsal stage it is not necessarily the flashes of artistic flair that will inspire amateur singers, but rather it will be the conductors' abilities to communicate the character of the music in an engaging and proficient manner. However, that is not to say that artistic flair has no place in the rehearsal room. Craft skills and craft knowledge are about how we communicate the essential in an efficient, musical, and human-compatible manner.

HUMAN-COMPATIBLE CONDUCTING

A common caricature of the conductor is of an elderly white male standing on a podium in tails waving a baton and looking somewhat severe. This reflects the view that the conductor's role is to dictate the music's requirements to the performers in an uncompromising way, responding to inaccurate pitches and rhythms sternly and not allowing poor intonation to escape his notice. Accounts of famous conductors identify a number of conductors for whom such a characterization fits. Discussion with many singers will also support this stereotype, with stories of bad temper, bullying, and abusive behavior among conductors being common. A solo singer friend of mine recalled a number of choral conductors who, during final rehearsals before concerts, behaved badly, showing their frustration by shouting and getting unnecessarily steamed up. The response from the singers to such behavior, he noticed, was invariably inhibited singing, forced tone, and considerable tension. Such a rehearsal atmosphere is not conducive to making music, being creative, or developing aesthetic sensitivities. Such a style of rehearsing could be said to be *antagonistic* to a learning or music-making condition.

A good conductor should be concerned with creating conditions in which, through careful manipulation and learning-compatible behavior, the singers can experience the sense of the music. It is more likely that this will occur if conductors are not preoccupied with technical accuracy at the early stage of rehearsals, especially with amateur or less confident singers. The concept of just "note bashing" or "*trying* to get things right" to start with may simply reinforce singers' feelings of inability or insecurity, as we have discovered in chapter 2, although we should be aware of allowing consistent errors to remain programmed in our singers' bodyminds. *Trying* can be a negative action; let's *do* by setting goals to achieve. Preferably, conductors will offer insight into the music's expressive character that will be recognized by the singers, and relevant patterns will be identified, thus opening up the pleasure centers of the bodymind. The technical aspects of the music might preferably be dealt with when the singers themselves realize that in order to gain further mastery over the music they require further information and correction. This is the essence of the conductors' craft in the rehearsal. The motivation to gain mastery is stronger when a person has previously received sensations that are pleasurable.

One of the conductor's roles is to help people overcome conscious controlling mechanisms that may well prevent them from using their other-than-conscious capabilities to develop mastery. Therefore, conductors need to know how humans tick. In their beguiling book *The

Inner Game of Music, Barry Green and Tim Gallwey outline such an approach. The authors point out that in order to gain maximum benefits from anything we do, there should be awareness of:

- the quality of our experience while we are doing it
- what we are learning as we do it
- how close we are coming to achieving our goals[10]

By focusing more closely on feelings while engaged in a learning situation, sensitivity to received feedback is heightened, according to Green and Gallwey. The heightened sensitivity in turn motivates the learner and quickens the learning rate, and performance goals are achieved and consequently enjoyment enhanced.

Leslie Hart, in *Human Brain and Human Learning,* emphasizes the importance of feedback in order that learners may "find out whether their pattern extraction and recognition is correct or improving, and whether programs have been appropriately selected and executed"[11] (see the discussion of high quality feedback in chapter 2). The responsibility of teachers and conductors is not only to provide a positive environment in which learning can take place, but also to provide feedback. Singers can improve individually and collectively when they have some way of knowing what has been done well through immediate feedback; the brain then builds and stores programs to repeat this behavior. Hart concludes: "Brain-compatible instruction requires that students *not* be permitted to pursue wrong programs at the outset, nor to practice making errors."[12] By allowing inaccurate or inappropriate practices to continue, the brain will be programmed accordingly, making it increasingly difficult to modify this behavior at a later stage.

Claire McCoy, writing in the *Choral Journal* about applying the theories of eurythmics to teacher training, emphasizes the importance of the quality of human interaction in the choral rehearsal. She points out that conductors have a responsibility to mold the musical performance through accurate and efficient gestures and words, and that this is achieved by recognizing the human element in leading a group of singers: "A more productive and congenial rehearsal climate is maintained when the conductor regards singers not as mere sound sources, but as human beings with musical, physical and emotional needs, strengths and limitations."[13] McCoy suggests that choral conductors must be skilled in building appropriate feelings in the rehearsal situation. Conductors have the responsibility then to enable singers to overcome their own obstacles in order to bring quality to the learning experience in singing. This must be an integral and substantial component of the model of effectiveness in choral training and conducting.

6

TOWARD A SUPER-MODEL CHORAL CONDUCTOR

Biographical accounts of conductors' lives offer various views and interpretations of what makes for good conducting (see chapter 4). Research findings and literature in the field also offer clues.[1] From these sources and from my own research I developed three categories to serve as a start in moving toward that model conductor:

- Philosophical principles
- Musical-technical skills
- Interpersonal skills

PHILOSOPHICAL PRINCIPLES

Some questions: Why am I a conductor? In many ways this question can be asked of anyone in relation to his or her chosen profession or activity: Why am I a teacher? Why am I a builder, a sailor, or a politician? Why do I think I am able to stand in front of singers and lead them in singing activity? Is it just that I have a set of particular musical skills, or just have the gumption to do it? (I do know of people who put themselves forward as conductors, albeit in an amateur capacity, who have little skill in conducting or rehearsing. So why do they do it?) Moreover, do I have a belief in myself as a conductor? Do I possess an understanding of appropriate choral and vocal issues? Do I have sufficient knowledge of the music, its style, its context, and its expressive character? Am I able to make appropriate decisions concerning the choice of music for the choir and its rehearsal and performance? Do I know what I am aiming for? And do I know when I have achieved it?

In the previous chapters, we have outlined some of the philosophical issues facing the choral conductor. Choral conductors need a fundamental belief in the integrity and value of music and singing. They will recognize that they have the wherewithal to influence people's commitment and aesthetic response to music. Conducting is more than mowing the lawn: the responsibilities of conductors include thoughtful preparation philosophically and psychologically of their role in relation to the singers.

Linked with these principles are the conductor's preparation of and approach to the music before rehearsals, in order to present to the singers its technical, expressive, and aesthetic qualities. Other more didactic texts refer to score preparation, giving strategies for learning the music. Here we will approach the issue more broadly. What it is to "know" a musical score is complex. Is it forming a mental visual image of the pages of musical notation, an inner aural image of the required sound, or an insight into the composer's structural and expressive intentions—or some combination of all three of these strategies? It is clearly useful to know the notes in terms of pitches and rhythms and how they fit into the harmonic structure. But there is more. To know a score for conducting purposes is to acquire elements of mental and aural images with reference to the composer's intentions. This goes far beyond what is written on the page of the score: that's just black blobs on paper. Tonal imagery is an image the conductor possesses of the *quality* of the sound in addition to the accuracy of pitches and rhythms.

Take, for example, the opening of Bruckner's motet *Locus Iste*. Forming an image of how the balance of the choral voices *should* sound will enable conductors to match *actual* sound heard in the rehearsal with their tonal image. Just stop for a moment and look at the opening of *Locus Iste*. What are you hearing, imagining, and bringing to mind?

Experienced conductors will have an image of the spacing of the chord, even possibly hear it at its actual pitch. They will have a preconceived notion of the tempo (it is so easy to get an unsuitable tempo for this piece), the required timbre, and the shaping of the first phrase with perhaps a subtle expansion of the long held chords. They will be able, with experience, to listen and adjust the balance and tonal quality accordingly through gesture and imagery. A bright sunrise over the Austrian Alps is an image that might help to convey the breathtaking freshness of the opening chord of *Locus Iste*. Certainly presenting images like this works for me in my rehearsals, because it is so easy to make this piece sound plodding, lifeless, and dull. The creation of appropriate kinesthetic as well as visual imagery and gesture will facilitate a bodymind condition in the singers, which in turn will enhance and preserve the distinct major tonality in the intonation, for example, of the first and fourth bars. My own experience tells me that providing an imaginative and creative approach using imagery in relation to musical intentions is effective and productive.

Knowledge of the workings of the voice and of how psychologically to deal with the singers in the rehearsal situation will determine the intonation of the opening phrase. Conductors will need to be able to hear the tuning, match it to their inner image, and explore appropriate strategies and helpful gestures, perhaps by rehearsing with particular vowel sounds, for example, in order to focus the sound. All this requires a philosophical underpinning that includes formal musical knowledge and skill, but also includes the craft knowledge and a knowing-in-action (see chapter 5).

The ability of conductors to deal with the technical aspects of the music is naturally important, because this addresses elements like accuracy of rhythm and pitch and vocal production. Equally important is an understanding of the music in its historical, stylistic, and textural contexts that can bring the music to life. How expressiveness can be presented within its stylistic context is essentially a reflective and aesthetic question that should be the concern of choral conductors before the first rehearsal. Dealing with the expressive character and style of the music from the start will stimulate, not get in the way of, the learning of its technical aspects. Ability to communicate these aesthetic principles must surely underpin the conductors' work at any level, in schools, churches, the wider amateur community, and among professional singers.

Deryck Cooke's *The Language of Music*[2] shows how, over the centuries, certain melodic, harmonic, and rhythmic elements have been codified into what might be described as a musical vocabulary. He attributes extramusical meanings to particular musical shapes showing how composers have intended meaning by using such shapes. We can illustrate this by examining the final movement of Verdi's *Requiem*. Pick up a score of the Verdi or, if not at hand, refer to any other piece with a gorgeous musical climax. Here is an example (between rehearsal figure **112** and **114** in the Ricordi vocal score, beginning with the text: 'Dum veneris judicare saeculum per ignem')[3] of how a musical climax is built by the

judicious use of crescendo, accelerando, and delay in order to emphasize the momentous musical and emotional peak. Not all performance
indications are supplied by Verdi in the score, however. Therefore the
conductor has to be aware of the structure and potential of the music in
order to convey its drama, tensions, resolutions, and expressive dimensions, and to acknowledge the technical demands that the soprano soloist
and the chorus will encounter. Verdi reveals musical meaning through
musical structures. We could well apply these principles to climaxes in
other musical examples.

Randall Gill draws some connections between aesthetic theories in relation specifically to the choice and understanding of choral literature.[4]
He outlines the basic principles of aesthetics using the terms *contextu-
alism, isolationism,* and *relativism* (Bennett Reimer's *referentialism, for-
malism,* and *expressionism*). To the *contextualist,* all music has meaning
outside the music itself, extramusical meaning or significance, as illus-
trated by Cooke. Clearly, for the choral conductor the emphasis on text
already gives music a meaning outside its formal structural language.
This directs the choral conductor to the musical meaning more obviously and more easily perhaps than for the orchestral conductor. The
isolationist approach is, however, to appreciate the music entirely from
its musical form. It is the structural and sound aspects of music that
inspire, regardless of text; it is the musical sounds to which we respond
aesthetically. The *relativist* position adopts the premise that musical language, form, and expression reflect our emotional lives. For example, is
the *Dona nobis pacem* of Bach's *Mass in B minor* a powerful and sublime movement essentially because of the meaning of the words of the
text—"grant us peace"—or because of the wonderfully crafted counter-
point? Or is it that it reflects something touching in our own emotional
or spiritual lives?

Could we sing the same music to the words of "How much is that dog-
gie in the window?" and elicit the same aesthetic response?[5] Handel used
material from his own and others' secular operas and instrumental compositions and transplanted them into his sacred oratorios. An example
of this is seen in the chorus *His yoke is easy* from *Messiah,* which is based
significantly on one of his Italian chamber duets. However, in terms of
aesthetic response, it must be the judicious combination of words and
music that elicits our response, as well as the context in which the music
is performed. The poignancy of the text of Bach's *Dona nobis pacem* for
me was never more so than when singing it at the end of a Christmas
concert after the terrorist attacks of September 11, 2001.

Choral conductors need to be aware of the significance of texts, particularly in certain contexts. Some texts, however beautifully set, somehow
appear inappropriate in the twenty-first-century choral environment. I

cannot myself, for example, be wholly convinced about the poetry set by Vaughan Williams in his *Sea Symphony;* it somehow seems dated for today's audiences and choirs in spite of the beautiful music. But his *Serenade to Music* is entirely convincing and exquisitely crafted with its text from Shakespeare's *The Merchant of Venice.* While *Rule Britannia* is indeed stirring stuff, can we really sing this imperialistic text seriously in post-empire European Britain? The words "Britons never shall be slaves" might sound pious, jingoistic, and insensitive, considering Britain's role historically in the slave trade. My personal view influences my program planning with choirs that I conduct (much to the chagrin of some singers). Others might argue that such music is a significant part of our cultural heritage and should not be ignored: these are equally convincing arguments.

MUSICAL-TECHNICAL SKILLS

Research shows—and it almost goes without saying—that a choral conductor's musicianship (defined as the manifestation of particular musical skills, knowledge, and sensitivity) is of vital importance. Aural perception and auditory acuity are essential attributes of a competent musician in a rehearsal situation. A number of writers and researchers on the subject suggest that a conductor must be able to identify inaccuracies and problems quickly and deal with them efficiently. (We should remember, though, that this is not the be-all and end-all of rehearsing, even though some conductors may think it is.) These skills are contingent on knowing the music and being able to relate what is heard in rehearsal to what is written in the score: moving toward the goal, taking target practice, aiming for the bull's-eye.

A research study by Crowe showed that error-detection skills were more reliable in conducting students when they had studied the score alongside correct aural examples than when they used other score preparation means.[6] He also found that students' error detection skills became less reliable as the number or parts in the musical examples increased. I suppose that is hardly surprising; if you have ever conducted Tallis's 40-part motet *Spem in alium* you will be severely challenged to hear all 40 independent vocal lines clearly and accurately! Crowe's study nevertheless implies that aural training using actual aural musical examples will benefit conducting students, and that contextualized aural training (that is in the context of rehearsing real music) is more effective than with dry isolated examples.

Aural skills are not, however, just concerned with detection of errors in rehearsals and accurate demonstration of the correct way to perform a passage, but also with the detection of stylistic inappropriateness, such as the use of liberal vibrato in a Purcell verse anthem. Awareness of and response to what is happening aurally in the choir is key. Some conductors have an inflexible plan of a rehearsal that does not respond to what the choir is actually producing. An auditioning conducting student started a rehearsal of Bach's motet *Lobet den Herrn* with our university choir by working on the German diction and pronunciation before having heard a note of the choir singing in German. While attention to diction and pronunciation is entirely appropriate, this particular choir's German was well practiced already and in pretty good shape. She did not respond to what the choir needed, or to what she had heard, because she hadn't heard anything! Responding to the outcomes of the singing is a craft skill that requires cultivation.

The technical skills of conducting and the effective use of conducting gesture is central to the attainment of required musical goals. Many performers are quick to be critical of any lack of clarity in conducting gesture. If ambiguity arises in the shape, direction, or movement of the beat, problems of ensemble are likely to arise. However, gesture goes beyond beating time, but becomes an essential ingredient in the conveyance of the expressive character of music. Conductors need to identify the several ways, for example, of conducting four beats in a bar, and be able to distinguish the appropriateness of the shape of the beat in relation to the character of music. Tallis's small anthem *If Ye Love Me* requires a different sort of "four in a bar" than Dawson's arrangement of the spiritual *Ev'ry Time I Feel the Spirit,* for example, or even from Erb's arrangement of *Shenandoah.* (I will deal with conducting gesture more extensively in chapter 8.)

Certain conducting gestures are actually inappropriate even though they might be held to be technically correct. An example here might be the use of excessive movement in a musical passage that is intended to be quiet and reflective. This would likely give an inappropriate message about the character of the music, even though the actual conducting beat may be clear. The connection between conducting and energy flow supports a kinesthetic approach to gesture rationalization that will have a bearing on the quality of vocal response from the singers. A taut attacking gesture at the beginning of, say, the Hallelujah chorus from *Messiah* will be reflected in a taut, probably tense sound from the singers, whereas a gesture that opens and allows the singer to *release* the sound will sound more open and released (more in chapter 8).

My colleague and friend Therees Hibbard further explored the kinesthetic approach to choral conducting and to the teaching of student conductors, with her case study and analysis of conductors' and singers' physical movements as an instructional technique for improving vocal production and expressive singing.[7] Singing can be enhanced by the judicious use of particular movements to capture a flowing phrase, reach a high note, create a particular vocal timbre, or heighten a rhythmic pattern (more on this in the context of rehearsing in chapter 7 and conducting gesture in chapter 8). This is the essence of kinesthesia—feeling through movement—which, as mentioned in chapter 2, is an underused and undervalued sense in Western classical musical culture.

Simple experiments in my conducting classes in the United Kingdom, United States, and South Korea, for example, have shown to student conductors that it is almost impossible for anyone to sing quietly and in a sustained legato style if the conductor is beating aggressively, jerkily, and expansively. Getting the students to sing a gentle sustained legato while conducting aggressively is a worthwhile and quick learning experience.

INTERPERSONAL SKILLS

Remember that we perceive all experiences through our visual, auditory, and kinesthetic senses. For "prominent visual processors" (those who file their experiences primarily through the visual sense), response to the conducting gesture will be uppermost. We can tell when conductors are committed to their choirs and to the music they are rehearsing and conducting by a variety of mostly non-verbal means. Facial expressions, eyes lighting up, the gestures and movements of the body all contribute to the message that may be received outside conscious awareness. This suggests that we might need more rigorous examination of the behavioral and communication skills aspects of conducting, as they are, in many ways, essential to successful musical and learning outcomes. It is largely the communication skills of conductors that will ensure successful exchange of information for effective rehearsals and performances.

R. Watkins carried out a descriptive study of choral directors working with their high school choirs, with particular regard to their use of modeling, metaphorical language, musical and technical language, and the relationship with student attentiveness.[8] He found that the majority of time in the observed rehearsals was spent on instruction using musical-technical language as opposed to using analogy and imagery—metaphorical language. However, when *less* time was spent on verbal instruction, the students were generally *more* attentive. This is very significant! Communication skills, such as pacing, timing, humor, enthusiasm, and a whole host of attributes are, in themselves, the properties of a good teacher. Watkins's findings support my belief that certain styles and strategies of communication motivate people, in this case the use of imagery and analogy, as opposed to an over-indulgence in the technical, which doesn't.

In order to identify and somehow measure teaching styles, Alan Gumm made an empirical study on the interaction of teaching behaviors and teaching style.[9] He refers to conducting "magnitude" to indicate levels of successful communication with students. Interpreting this for the choral conductor in the rehearsal setting, high-magnitude conducting involves:

- maintaining eye contact throughout the rehearsal
- keeping close proximity to the students
- using an enthusiastic variation in voice volume
- using a great variety of gestures
- using appropriate and contrasting facial expressions
- keeping the pace rapid and exciting

At the other end of the scale (as one might expect) low-magnitude conducting involves:

- never looking at singers
- remaining behind the music stand away from the singers
- using an unenthusiastic voice
- using restricted conducting gestures
- keeping a neutral facial expression
- keeping the rehearsal slow and methodical

If we wish to establish an expressive and aesthetically stimulating rehearsal, low-magnitude conducting will not help. Eye contact is everything; if conductors can make eye contact (and smile) with individuals during rehearsals and performance, those individuals are more likely to feel involved in the event. Eyes fixed on the score, or eyes alive with the music and sharing it? Remaining aloof and behind a music stand all the time (OK, I know we have to in performance!) will create barriers; moving toward groups of people can be an effective way again of making them feel you are attending to them. Think of the conductors who have inspired you, about what it was that took your breath away or made you really want to sing for them. A conductor with a slow, plodding, predictable style of rehearsing and conducting probably won't be the model conductor you envision, whereas one with an enthusiastic, brisk-paced, and less predictable style of rehearsing and conducting will more likely fit.

As part of my ongoing research in this field, I held a number of interviews with singers from a successful choir in Finland. The group, a "living choir" as described by one of its singers, has a particular reputation for singing contemporary Finnish music, some of which is improvisatory as well as challenging musically and expressively. Their conductor is clearly successful and very committed, and had developed a special relationship with the singers over a period of eight or so years. One notable comment from the singers was that the eyes of the conductor conveyed the expression required in their singing: the eyes "radiated" her enthusiasm and passion. My daughters had the fabulous opportunity a few years ago as instrumentalists in the local youth orchestra of being rehearsed and conducted by Simon Rattle. The difference in the sound of the orchestra when he conducted was remarkable. When I asked what it was that he did, both girls indicated that he caught their eye and *enticed* them to play. They *wanted* to play for him.

Vocal timbre is part of the modeling of expressiveness. How can conductors speak in an unenthusiastic voice and expect something dynamic to happen in the voices of the singers? Excitement or passion for music can be portrayed in the speaking as well as vocalizing timbres of the conductor, in the same way the excitement and passion for music can be represented visually with conducting gesture and facial expression. Pacing and timing of rehearsals is part of the craft of conducting and teaching that motivates singers and maintains their interest.

Other research studies in music teaching styles have found that students respond and progress more favorably with extroverted teachers, suggesting that in a conducting context this might be a useful trait to adopt. Clearly, I am not suggesting that there is a kind of stereotype conductor that we want to clone, but rather that certain kinds of behaviors and interpersonal skills will promote learning and, in our case, expressive and dynamic singing. Can some of these behaviors and skills be taught? I hope so!

THE MODEL OF AN EFFECTIVE CHORAL CONDUCTOR

My model of an effective choral conductor emerges from the body of research and other literature in music and general education, as well as my own research through observations and interviews over a period of years. I have consciously promoted the notion that conductors should operate as teachers, not just as instructors, rather as promoters of learning—"senior learners"—to use Jerome Bruner's term. This can be achieved in any context by providing conducive learning experiences through the creation of positive environments and appropriate and high quality feedback. More specific practical applications—modes and styles of rehearsing, gesture, verbal and non-verbal language and actions—will be further explored and evaluated in relation to the emerging model in following chapters.

This model might suggest that we are aiming to create a superman or superwoman of the conducting world. But at least the model could provide us with something to aim for, because most of us are still Batman's Robin, or the Sorcerer's apprentice. A model is after all only a model. For those teaching conducting, it might prepare the way for a curriculum that goes beyond the notes in the score (see chapter 10).

Are we any nearer an understanding of the dynamic interaction and connection that conductors are potentially able to provide? I don't believe as choral conductors we can be inspiring and dynamic in every rehearsal situation. However, we can work toward acquiring the skills, attributes, and conditions necessary for such quality singing experiences to be more likely to happen. So, the model conductor will have:

Philosophical Principles Underpinning Role

- **a knowledge of the choral repertoire** in order to be able to choose music that is appropriate for the particular choral group, in respect of their age, abilities, composition, and vocal needs, from a wide range of eras and styles
- **a knowledge of the human voice** in order to be able to deal with a range of vocal issues and problems in an informed way in the rehearsal situation, including aspects of vocal production, healthy voice use, and the psychology, physiology, and workings of the voice to promote better and effective singing
- **an image of the music prior to rehearsal** in order to have clear technical and expressive ideas for presenting it to the singers
- **an awareness of the aesthetic potential of the music** including the composer's intentions, the import of the text, and the capacity to enable appropriate responses in the singers and the audience to emerge
- **an understanding of the nature of the conductor's role** to take responsibility for the singers collectively and individually, and to act as a facilitator and promoter of appropriate musical learning

---

Musical-Technical Skills

- **appropriate aural and error detection skills** in order to be able to hear what is going on, including inaccuracies in the singing, such as inaccurate entries, pitches, rhythms; also identify problems in language, diction, vowel shapes, and textural nuances, endings of phrases, intonation, blend, balance within and among parts, and to be able to deal with them

- **the ability to give clear intentions of tempo, dynamics, phrasing through appropriate gesture** including clear preparatory beats, cutoffs, as well as conducting gestures that indicate suitable expressive and stylistic considerations; also ability to achieve rhythmic energy, agility, and spontaneity within the musical structure
- **the ability to demonstrate accurately and musically,** which will involve singing and/or playing at appropriate pitches and rhythms; also tonal quality and intonation for the singers to hear and emulate; it might also include demonstrating how *not* to do something
- **recognition of the importance of warming up voices,** of knowing and delivering strategies appropriate for the group, and the validity of physical and vocal exercises in relation to physical and vocal preparation for effective singing and rehearsing and vocal health
- **strategies for establishing the character of the music at the earliest opportunity** in order not to put undue emphasis on technical considerations at the expense of expressive and stylistic ones

Interpersonal Skills

- **the capacity to create a positive non-threatening environment** with a balance of encouragement, praise, and adjustment, with realistic, attainable goals and high-quality feedback in a "safe" atmosphere
- **the capacity to communicate clearly and unambiguously** with effective use of verbal, gestural, body, and facial language
- **the desire to encourage healthy singing** through avoidance of situations with language (including the use of conductor's own voice) and gestures that will induce tension, but rather maintain an emphasis on relaxation
- **the capacity to enable choral and vocal development,** the skill to assist with voice and choral blend, allowing individual vocal exploration, and the careful use of extroverted behavior to motivate singers
- **the ability to make singers feel confident and comfortable** with reassuring language, allowing inaccuracies and taking target practice, using human-compatible communication and a judicious use of humor

- **the skill to pace rehearsals effectively,** including using verbal language sparingly and encouraging response to visual cues by various means, and avoiding concentrating on one section of the group while others become bored or demotivated
- **the expectation of the highest standards possible** by renewing expectations, setting appropriate goals for the group, particularly the development of musical and textural communication from the singers, and giving high-quality feedback to the choir

The model is not an absolute one, and, although attributes have been categorized, there will be a degree of cross-fertilization among and within them. Nevertheless, the model presents, if you like, a new philosophy of choral conducting and ends the first part of the book. Now I shall address some aspects of the choral conducting phenomenon to put the model into practice.

II

Practice

7

THE CONDUCTORS' CRAFT: REHEARSING

Concentrate on the music instead of the problem; you
could be in for a pleasant surprise.

George, an American friend, telephoned me one evening when I was staying in a hotel in Atlanta. He is a singer and choral conductor himself and was taking part in a singing course led by two "eminent" choral conductors, one English and one American. He was somewhat perturbed to report that there were two distinct styles of choral training and rehearsing in evidence. One of the conductors was making the singers feel confident and encouraged by their efforts, while the other spent a large proportion of the rehearsal time castigating the choir for not knowing the notes, thus creating a feeling of insecurity and negativity among the singers. While both had high standing in the choral conducting fraternity, one made my friend feel good and the other made him feel bad. The psychological impact of the rehearsal situation was dynamic. With another, perhaps less experienced singer, the result might have been more significant. George was able to handle and analyze the situation more objectively; he was a conductor himself and knew that he was able to motivate and encourage his own choirs effectively. However, he had learned a salutary lesson from this particular experience, which supported his own intuitive thinking on the importance of creating an appropriate atmosphere in the choral rehearsal environment.

Another anecdote comes from an opera singer friend who reported being conducted by someone in a professional context (so no names here!). She was struggling somewhat with a passage from *La Bohème*, and the conductor was clearly becoming increasingly irritated: it showed in his facial expressions. After a while, the conductor, seemingly exasperated with the situation, demanded of the soprano, "Why can't you sing this beautifully?" She replied, "How can I possibly sing this beautifully when you are making such an ugly face?" The lesson again is salutary; the fact that this conductor expected the singer to sing beautifully while making an ugly facial expression himself is simply going against human nature. We respond to what we see. If someone smiles at us, we are more likely to smile back. If we scowl at someone, the response is hardly likely to be a smile. In this case, the conductor failed to make the bodymind connection, the "human-compatible connection" if you like. Imagine that conductor with less confident singers. Conductors cannot just *demand* beautiful singing; it has to be nurtured and created by aesthetically appropriate gesture and communication.

In talking to various people and especially my own students, I am forever being given examples of conductors who have made singers feel uncomfortable, inadequate, and insecure about their singing and musical abilities. One student reported that she had observed one conductor verbally abuse his choir repeatedly over a period of time. He used to lose his temper regularly, and the singers appeared to accept that this was normal, acceptable behavior for conductors in rehearsals. It was as if the singers needed to come back week after week just to suffer this humiliation—as if it were good for them! The subliminal expectation was that conductors will and should get angry with their choirs.

Asking people about their own perceptions of their singing ability can supply further evidence of the psychological impact of conductors' behavior. It is regrettably not uncommon to find someone who believes that he or she cannot sing or is tone-deaf. This is probably due to some careless comment made at a formative time in their lives, during childhood or adolescence, perhaps; such a comment can have lasting damage on a person's singing life. Particularly in amateur groups and contexts where people attend to sing in a voluntary capacity, the rehearsal is the time for learning and developing individually and collectively, musically, vocally, and socially. These social and psychological aspects of the choral singing phenomenon cannot be ignored (see chapter 3).

While there can be no blueprint for an effective choral rehearsal, a set of strategies and techniques can be developed for those who wish to maximize their efficiency and effectiveness in the rehearsal situation. The model provided at the end of chapter 6 is a philosophical or theoretical one, so this and following chapters will propose and outline its practical application.

The rehearsal is as important as the performance and ideally should not be treated just as preparation for a concert performance, but as a musical and social event in its own right with its own integrity. The thrust of each rehearsal will depend on the context—whether it is a choir of young children, senior citizens, a village church choir, or a large urban choral society. It will depend on whether this is the first rehearsal of a new term or the last rehearsal before a major performance. A rehearsal can also be influenced by outside events. I recall rehearsing my community choir on the evening of the Dunblane tragedy: earlier that day, Thomas Hamilton had entered a primary school in the little Scottish town and shot 28 children, 16 fatally, and killed their teacher before turning the gun on himself. Such an incredible incident had contributed to an overwhelming tension throughout the evening that was difficult to diffuse. Even hundreds of miles away in London, the tragedy of the day had affected people more than they could understand or articulate. The members of the choir had to be helped to deal with their emotions through the music being rehearsed.

A chapter on choral rehearsing can become a prescriptive list of "what to do" and "what not to do." However, I shall attempt to outline some principles that, through research, teaching, observation, and experience, have proved invaluable in moving toward a model of effective choral rehearsing and conducting and therefore a positive musical encounter and effective communication. It is impossible to cover everything, but the main areas considered in this section of the book will be:

- creating the environment
- creating the atmosphere
- warm-ups
- planning and preparation
- verbal and non-verbal language
- movement in the choral rehearsal
- spacing and acoustics
- intelligent rehearsing

These areas are clearly related, and I cannot deal satisfactorily with any of them in isolation from the others. Consequently, these sections should not be read without recognition and acceptance of the holistic view of choral conducting effectiveness that, I hope, permeates the text.

CREATING THE ENVIRONMENT

The craft of the choral conductor is concerned with the day-to-day, week-by-week rehearsing that can often become quite humdrum and uninteresting. As with the instrumental music teacher who must guard against developing an unvarying pattern of established procedure in structuring lessons, so the choral conductor needs to beware of adopting an unvarying and prescriptive methodology and pattern of rehearsing that will fail to inspire or motivate the singers because of its predictability. Many conductors are able to interest and excite singers in a "one-off" event or rehearsal, and it is inspiring to have such workshops with different leaders and conductors from time to time. However, the regular rehearsal paradigm is the one that really tests the craft of the choral conductor. Some conductors as teachers in schools are expected to rehearse the choir after a hard day's teaching or while grabbing a sandwich in the lunch break. The conductors' evening battle through traffic to attend the choral society or church choir practice is not the ideal prelude to running an inspiring and effective rehearsal.

In ideal situations, conductors would have time to relax and prepare themselves mentally, physically, and emotionally for the demands of the ensuing rehearsal. They would have time to "warm up" physically and vocally before expecting the choir to do the same. And conductors would be able to plan and prepare the rehearsal in order to make the most efficient and effective use of the rehearsal time as appropriate for the choir. However, most of us live in the real world, and such ideal situations are normally hard to come across. But the efficiency and effectiveness of a rehearsal with a conductor who is musically and mentally prepared will show.

When I was consulting for the music department of a secondary school in London some years ago, I observed a choir rehearsal during the lunch break. The students and some teachers arrived at and left the rehearsal at different times. Some (including the conductor) were eating and drinking during the rehearsal. The singers were sitting anywhere—on tables in a slumped posture or on chairs in no particular placing—and tackling music that was actually too demanding for them. They seemed to be a small, committed group of people, but I remarked afterward that the subliminal message was one that suggested that choir was not a priority. It was "slotted in" somehow and was thus perceived as being not really important. While I recognize all the difficulties in a school schedule and particularly the conflicting demands that prevent singers from getting together in an extracurricular context, this was really not a satisfactory or productive environment for anyone, the singers or the conductor. If a school expects to have a choir that performs at public functions, it needs to be perceived as a priority in everyone's schedule.

Another primary school music teacher told me how she found it impossible to run a choir at the end of the school day because the children were tired and there were often conflicts with other activities and appointments. She eventually decided that choir rehearsals should take place at 8 o'clock in the morning. The result was entirely positive; she created choir as a priority in the lives of the children, so much so that after the first ten minutes they were not admitted late to the rehearsal. The singing, attendance, and attitude improved markedly. The environment became focused and serious, and much better singing was achieved.

CREATING THE ATMOSPHERE

Are the smiles on the flight attendants' faces as you board the aircraft genuine? They may be socially fabricated smiles; after all, they are instructed to greet you warmly in order to encourage you to fly again, but also they want to make you, and particularly the nervous traveler, comfortable. Just imagine being greeted as you board with a grunt or look of displeasure; that would be very unnerving for some.

It may seem unnecessary to say, but the way a teacher walks into a classroom, or a conductor walks into the rehearsal room, matters. After all, the people who come into a choir rehearsal room are about to expose something of their inner selves; they cannot hide behind an instrument—the precious voice *is* their instrument—and the less confident singer is vulnerable musically, psychologically, and emotionally. The way we greet people—with a smile or a glare, or not at all—affects the atmosphere we create. Do we make eye contact with people? Do we suggest by our body language that we would rather be somewhere else? Do we look interested and excited by the fact that it is rehearsal time? And this is before a note of music has been sung.

In his book *Nonverbal Communication,*[1] Albert Mehrabian, a psychologist at the University of California, proposed that 45 percent of communication is transmitted vocally while 55 percent is transmitted by facial expression, arm-hand gestures, and postural arrangements of the body. Of the 45 percent of vocally transmitted communication, Mehrabian suggests that only 7 percent is perceived and produced "in conscious awareness" of verbal content, whereas 38 percent is nearly always perceived and produced "outside conscious awareness," as part of the non-verbal context of spoken communication. This is achieved through variations of vocal pitch, volume, timbre, and timing and pacing of speech. These communications are the ones that drive and shape our feelings—"feeling meanings," if you like.

We might take a moment to look at how babies respond not to literal meanings of words, but rather to "connotative" meanings. They interpret sounds as comforting or distressing through the pitch contours, timbre, and volume of the parents' voices, not through the "denotative" meanings. These affect the feelings of the baby—feeling meanings—especially of safety or uncertainty, in which their responses will be particularly acute. How many of us have responded to the cries of our own young babies with frustration because we did not understand why they were crying, or even with anger, which did not help the situation one jot? They sensed the frustration or anger and continued to show distress; how could they possibly know otherwise?

Mehrabian's research is therefore significant for conductors and teachers also. How much do we convey our mood and feelings when entering a room, for example? Do we rely exclusively on verbal instruction to transmit our intentions? Singers can sense when a conductor is in a bad mood at the beginning of the rehearsal, not just through hearing speech, but by observing the facial expression, the deliberate walk to the podium, noticing the lack of eye contact, the way the scores are placed on the music stand. Then, of course, the manner in which the conductor says "Let's start from the opening of the piece" will shape the feeling meanings of the singers. All these are communications that convey a message to the awaiting singers, and that message is interpreted emotionally. The singers may be more guarded—they don't want to upset the conductor further—and therefore more reserved in their disposition to the rehearsal. The consequence will be less efficient and less effective singing, because our emotional makeup is intimately connected with our singing, as we have discovered in earlier chapters. While carefully chosen and incremental warm-ups are important, so too is the attitude of conductors and the way they create positive, safe learning environments in order to produce effective rehearsals and efficient and healthy singing.

At a choral rehearsal during a national convention some time ago, the conductor was rehearsing a choir made up of other choral conductors in a newly commissioned piece. The words of greeting were a reprimand to those arriving late, saying that this was not professional behavior. Unfortunately, he (a conductor of some supposed repute) set a somewhat antagonistic atmosphere and failed to gain the respect and loyalty of a number of the singers, and while being otherwise musically competent, he did not run a genial rehearsal. This is not to say that conductors should not expect choir members to arrive punctually, but rather to illustrate that, on this particular occasion, the first words for the very first rehearsal of this group of people were not judiciously chosen. Some delegates consequently chose not to attend further sessions with that conductor.

People join choirs for a variety of reasons, but a principal motive is that people wish to identify with and belong to a group (see chapter 3).

Threatening gesture.

Safe gesture.

Just look at the two photographs to decide which one creates a more enticing rehearsal environment. Which gesture and expression will be more likely to promote healthy singing?

A musical encounter can lift people out of their ordinary existence; musical encounter enables people to express emotions that cannot be expressed in any way other than singing. We also know that singing involves a sense of emotional release, in which a physiological response is created by a chemical reaction in the body involving the pleasure-producing neural networks that are part of the brain and nervous system. As a result, there is an increased release of endorphins, the body's natural pleasure-giving and pain-killing chemicals. Part of the conductors' role is to create the atmosphere in which people can feel good about the singing activity. Basic psychology will tell us that people will respond to challenge more efficiently if they experience pleasure sensations in the activity. The creation by conductors, therefore, of a positive, encouraging atmosphere is integral to this response to musical challenges.

WARM-UPS

It is not unusual for conductors to find that there is so much to get through in each rehearsal that pressure is on to get going as soon as possible, to "learn the notes." However, how much learning is actually occurring at the beginning of a rehearsal—before the singers (and conductors) are in an appropriate state of readiness mentally, physically, and vocally—is debatable. A number of choral educators put forward a convincing rationale for warming up the choir at the beginning of each rehearsal, arguing that it is time well used. These include mental, physical, vocal, emotional, and psychological warm-ups. In an ideal rehearsal situation all these aspects should be attended to with all the singers. My own strategies vary from rehearsal to rehearsal, but usually are concerned with:

- physical (stretching, massaging)
- focusing (getting singers to copy actions, for example; particularly useful for gaining the attention of children)
- breathing
- vocalizing (gradually extending vocal range with different vocal timbres; linking with music to be rehearsed)

A significant purpose of warm-ups at the beginning of rehearsals is to release tension. After a day's work, or an academic lesson for younger singers, there is a need to unwind a little before engaging in singing. Preparing the body and the voice is vital for efficient and effective voice use as well as rehearsal time. Physical stretching and massaging can create smiles and laughter, which will release tension, loosen muscles, and prepare the singers psychologically for the rehearsal. How much better it is to generate laughter at the start of a rehearsal rather than make people

Young singers stretch as part of warm-up.

feel awkward through some careless and possibly unnecessary admonition.

Some examples of physical warm-ups might include

- stretching the torso from side to side
- bending forward and allowing the back and head to flop loosely and slowly unfolding the back—with the head coming up last of all (probably more difficult for some older singers)
- gently massaging the shoulders and upper back and arms of another singer
- stretching arms and legs—raising arms in the air and releasing, also standing on tip-toe, stretching, and releasing
- massaging face; imagine and simulate biting into a sharp lemon followed by lying relaxed on a sun-drenched beach, in order to stretch and relax the face muscles
- slapping the surface body area to bring the blood to the surface and energize the singers; this is especially useful if singers have come in from the cold (some of us live in northern climes) or to revitalize singers toward the end of a tiring rehearsal.

Focus or mental warm-ups are particularly useful for gaining the attention of children, but singers of all ages are usually captivated by "follow-the-leader" activities. These can simply be finger clicks, rhythmic patterns and actions to be performed by conductor and singers simultaneously. (Of course, it is not necessary for the conductor always to lead these.) I often use these when working as a choral clinician in a "one-off" rehearsal with choirs that I meet for the first time: they all look! Other focus warm-ups might include call-and-response phrases: clapping or clicking rhythmic patterns or vocal ones. Again, it is a good idea to pass around the leadership role among the singers when they feel safe, letting them initiate short melodic or rhythmic phrases for the others to imitate.

Breathing warm-ups are an interesting concept. We all breathe in order to exist, but there are many ways in which we can be more efficient in our breathing, particularly when it comes to singing. As singing is an aerobic activity, breathing efficiently and effectively is paramount to good, expressive, and healthy singing. As we are all different shapes and sizes and all have varying body proportions, I prefer to avoid using the word *correct* to describe anything to do with singing.

There are certainly more *appropriate* and *less appropriate* ways of breathing in order to maintain efficiency. Some principles and examples of warm-ups include:

Breathing warm-up.

• Get singers to put their hands around the stomach as if holding it in. While taking a breath, they should allow the stomach and chest area to extend as if a *splat,* release the hands in the line of the stomach muscles—an ugly sight, I realize—but the shoulders will then naturally fall and relax. Exhale the air and pull the stomach in (this can be done on a variety of sounds *ssh...* or *phhh...* or counting, also at varying speeds and time). The action with the hands helps to internalize the feeling of the breathing space and cavity for expansion and pushes energy through the body and the vocal tract. The singers then concentrate on the stomach muscles and wholesome diaphragmatic breathing rather than the clavicular (short breaths from the upper torso also more likely to raise the shoulders). The photograph shows how conductors can encourage their singers to adopt gestures to ensure full breathing.

• Imagine ten-pin bowling. Ask singers to adopt the position (one foot in front of the other, knees relaxed and unlocked). When pulling the arm back with the imaginary bowl, the singers will naturally take in a breath from the diagphragm, then send the bowl down the alley with a long vocal *weeeeee...* across the full vocal range, including the falsetto range for the guys.

• When the principles of deep diaphragmatic breathing are established, then slow, sustained chords can be sung on any sound: I find the word *alleluia* a useful one with its different vowels to assist with vowel unity, or any other sounds. Get the singers to conduct with you, especially to hold and sustained the tone on long notes.

Thomas Hemsley in his book *Singing and Imagination* gives useful and singer-friendly advice on his approach to breathing. He suggests that breathing should be essentially natural and controlled by the whole body "with the strength centred in the lower belly, and guided by the singer's intention, stimulated by imagination."[2] He argues that breathing depends on the clear visualization and anticipation of what is to be sung. Think of the larger musical picture—the whole musical phrase—and singers will largely respond accordingly. He also comments that a natural good posture will enable efficient and effective breathing. But, suggests Hemsley, singers need to sense their entire bodies as resonators for stimulating vibration rather than as bellows for blowing out air. In essence, all breathing needs to be thought of in terms of the requirements of the music; it needs to be natural.

One helpful way of developing an appropriate posture (and therefore appropriate breathing) for singers is through physical stretching warm-ups to encourage flexible body movement. I also find this a useful exercise to do with conducting students. When supple, lean the whole body and

Breathing action with gestures.

head forward, bending down as far as possible from the waist. (You might want to recommend that those with back problems or elderly singers take care here.) Allow the head to become loose and floppy; let the body hang and keep knees unlocked and ankle joints flexible. Then gradually raise the body from the waist as if unfurling the spine with the head being raised last of all. Ask the singers (and conductors) then to stand in an appropriate and good singing, and therefore good conducting, posture (let them decide what appropriate and good is), with arms relaxed. Continue breathing in this "natural" posture, perhaps with the hands and arms as if holding a light but large beach ball if you want imaginative imagery. This posture will also help to expand the chest and abdominal regions and therefore maximize breathing potential.

Vocal warm-ups should really begin in the middle and comfortable vocal range, moving gently at first to get the vocal mechanism up and running. Think of this as an athletic warm-up. The range can then be extended as the singers warm up, so that if the music to be rehearsed is demanding in terms of vocal ranges, then the singers will be ready for that vocal challenge. Examples of vocalizes can be found in other sources, but it is advisable to include something that has reference to the music to be rehearsed. There may well be musical passages that present certain challenges for the singers that could effectively be dealt with during this warm-up period, without using the score, thus alleviating the problem of reading the notation. Singers are more likely to learn a tricky musical passage more effectively by listening to a vocal model and imitating, rather than being encumbered by reading the score as well. (I have proved this to myself and, I hope, to my choirs, many times.) Rehearsals at the beginning of the day will need special care and attention, as will those at the beginning of the year following a summer break. At these times, warm-ups should not be sacrificed at all, as the benefits will be manifest later.

Warm-ups can act as mechanisms for the development of specific choral issues. A common need in choirs, for example, is attention to vowel sounds. Vowels need to be unified in choral singing because the ugly sound of diphthongs can interfere with the musical expression. Words like *now, fire,* or *sound* can prove problematic aurally as they have diphthongs—that is, more than one pure vowel sound. The movement through the vowel sound itself will, likely as not, be inconsistent among the singers. (Korean, by the way, is a much cleaner language in which to sing because the vowels are pure.) Singing single repeated notes or chords on *mah, may, mee, moh, moo,* for example, or *ah-lay-loo-ya* (alleluia), will enable singers to give attention to vowel sounds and good tone production as well as act itself as a vocal warm-up.

Further examples and ideas for warm-ups can be found in *Group Vocal Technique* by Frauke Haasemann and James Jordan. They suggest that each choral rehearsal should "begin with general exercises which lead the choir through familiar concepts and attempts to create a body that is ready for singing. . . . It may also be the time to re-teach or reacquaint the choir with previously taught concepts, or to introduce new ones."[3] They also advocate using particular passages from the repertoire in order that the singers can make direct connections between the vocal technique being taught and its relationship with the music about to be sung. So, for example, the descending fifth interval at the beginning of the fugal entries in the chorus *And he shall purify* from *Messiah* can be formed into a vocal exercise with a sequence of descending fifths, moving down or up and in varying keys. Sometimes it is useful for conductors to anticipate vocal and technical challenges in a work and prepare them during the warm-ups. Scalic passages and runs, as in many baroque and classical movements, can typically be worked on without the score, as can aspects of diction, harmonic movement, rhythmic challenges, and a whole host of vocal techniques.

Other sources of warm-up ideas in relation to songs particularly geared to young singers can be found in Jo McNally's series *Junior Choral Club*,[4] and some useful information on vocal techniques in Mike Brewer's booklet *Kick-Start Your Choir*.[5]

PLANNING AND PREPARATION

The issue of planning and preparation is paramount, both for school music teachers in the classroom and for the choral rehearsal. Planning is concerned with

- repertoire, for the next concert term, the year, and the longer term; exploration of the aims and goals of the choir in collaboration with the singers, the committee, or head of department
- the series of rehearsals for the term or for the program
- individual rehearsals

The first point of planning is the choice of suitable repertoire for the group in question. One of the challenging jobs of the choral director, I find, is designing programs interesting to both the choir and the audience. While there may be opportunities on occasions to perform the great oratorios with orchestra and professional soloists, it is more usual for most choirs to have to produce smaller-scale items either in the school choir context or within the liturgical and worship context of a church service. Some limitations are already imposed upon choirs by the nature of their function. However, program planning is a complex job. Planning considerations will include

- the level of ability of the choir
- the balance and strengths of the vocal parts within the choir
- an interesting and perhaps contrasting repertoire within one program
- a repertoire to attract and challenge singers
- a program to appeal to an audience
- the concert venue, its space and acoustics
- the cost

While it is not possible to deal with all the considerations that each choral conductor will face in the planning of programs, I will set out some principles that should govern choice of repertoire. Clearly, individual choir directors have their own musical preferences that will shape the overall planning. Conductors need to be musically convinced by a work in order to be able to lead and inspire others in its rehearsal and performance. I recall Benjamin Britten saying in conversation that he was not particularly convinced by Mendelssohn's *Elijah* and so felt unable to conduct it. We remember, however, his utterly convincing performances of Mozart (I was privileged to sing in a compelling performance of the *Requiem* with Britten conducting) and much other music in addition to his own. While conductors should not just perform their favorite pieces, it is more likely that the singers will be convinced by music that the conductor "believes in." That is not to say conductors should not take risks and try new music and different musical styles and genres within their repertoire, but rather attitudes toward music, including those outside our conscious awareness, will permeate a rehearsal and transfer to the singers. Ideally, repertoire should reflect the canon of choral literature from the earliest Renaissance to contemporary and new compositions.

Music within appropriate vocal ranges is especially important to consider with young singers. Far too often music that is aimed at young singers is chosen (and published) that is pitched unsuitably. John Cooksey has carried out a great deal of research into the adolescent male changing voice and points out that choral directors should take great care with choosing material that suits the boys in their different voice stages. This research has critical implications, for example, for some of the traditional ways of operating within the British choral culture. Lynne Gackle has carried similar work in relation to the changing stages of the female adolescent voice (see chapter 9).

While the onus is on publishers and composers to provide schools and youth choirs with suitable material, it is also incumbent on teachers and choral conductors of such groups to choose repertoire with care. Choice of text can also influence the success and motivation of young singers. Whatever music is chosen, conductors should come to the first rehearsals with a clear image of the music, demonstrable knowledge of the individual voice parts in order to recognize inaccuracies, an understanding of the text, and insight into the expressive character and intentions of the composer.

Planning for the medium term—perhaps the series of rehearsals leading up to a concert performance—will be needed to ensure that all music programmed for a concert is covered and rehearsed adequately according to the level of its challenge. Singers will feel better and safer knowing that their conductor is well prepared and can be trusted to get them through all the music. In this medium-term context, planning of rehearsals will include revision of work previously covered as well as introduction of new material. It is usually better to start and finish each rehearsal with something that is known to show to the choir that they have achieved something. The bulk of new and detailed work is best done after an initial sing-through and certainly not at the very end. Singers need to start and finish feeling good about themselves and their singing. So, avoid tacking too much new material in a single rehearsal.

In individual rehearsals, variety of approach is key. I recently observed Chloe, a student choral conductor, in a middle school rehearsing a choir performing three pieces. In each piece, she took a small section and rehearsed specific detail without any reference to the pieces as a whole. So, for the 50-minute rehearsal the young singers had not sung through any of the pieces, and the singing itself distinctly lacked verve and excitement or any sense of the expressive character of each piece. At the end of the session, I suggested to Chloe that she should work only on one or maybe two pieces in detail, and that at least one piece should be sung through as much as possible in order to gain the feeling of the whole. My main concern was that the approach should not be the same for each piece in any one rehearsal. Chloe took to heart my suggestion and, observing the same group at the same time the following week, I noticed that the level of commitment from the singers was noticeably enhanced as they sang through the first piece, worked in detail on diction of a small extract from the second piece, and tackled some detail but also sang through most of the third. The quality of the experience was improved for both the singers and the student conductor; in addition, there was certainly more evidence of their understanding of the expressive character of the music.

Contrast the repertoire also in each rehearsal. Follow a boisterous song or movement with a slow, expressive one, or one that demands a different kind of singing and vocal quality. Follow a homophonic song with a polyphonic one, a sacred one with a secular or one in a different language. Like a meal with different courses, the expectation is that each course will have different and distinctive tastes to make the whole meal interesting, appetizing, and satisfying.

Decide on which details need to be covered in a particular rehearsal, and make sure that there is a balance between working hard on details and challenging pieces and singing through pieces that are easier on the voice and the brain. Working on too much intricate detail or "note bashing" in one rehearsal can become soul destroying for the unconfident singer. Make sure that each rehearsal finishes with something that has already been learned and sounds satisfying: psychologically this is important for singers' sense of achievement and self-esteem. It's the aromatic espresso or fine cognac at the end of a good meal.

The craft of rehearsing will be to know what can be achieved in each rehearsal and, supported by positive and encouraging remarks, to lead the singers toward the goal, the bull's-eye, while preferably avoiding negative comments or referring only to technical inaccuracies. We need to be encouraged to keep striving to get better and make sense of our musical world through singing activity.

Let us focus on a single rehearsal to illustrate how, by using a variety of strategies and approaches, we might keep singers motivated and on task and establish a human-compatible learning situation. This example is based on a recent two-hour rehearsal of Verdi's *Requiem* with my large community choir. It was my first rehearsal with them after an extended absence, although a colleague had started working with them on this program:

1. Series of warm-ups, using physical, mental, and vocal exercises. During the warm-up time, we rehearse (without referring to the scores, and starting on different pitches) the chant-like *Libera me, Domine, de morte aeterna* . . . at the beginning of the *Libera me* movement. Singers concentrate therefore on listening to me model the words and their inflections and focus on my conducting to feel the stress of the words and flow of the phrases. We also focus on intonation through the repeated notes. They gesture with me, unencumbered by the scores, which helps them to gain a kinesthetic insight into the music. This starts the vocalizing within a comfortable range for each voice part. Further vocalizes to extend ranges.

2. Sing through the opening *Requiem & Kyrie* stopping to point out the two subtle different rhythms on the words *et lux*

perpetua and *luceat eis* and rehearsing the difference. Run through the *Kyrie*, and check couple of bars that are causing the tenors some difficulty. Take these bars apart and put together with the alto, then the other parts.

3. Move on to sing through the opening section of the *Dies Irae*. This is a contrasting movement: some minor adjustments.

4. Work on the *Agnus Dei* movement, again a contrast from the previous one rehearsed. Here I ask the choir to sing small sections (the first being in unison) from memory, so that we can concentrate on the vocal tone and vowels as well as breathing and the shaping of the phrases. We spend quite a bit of time on this movement; although it is seemingly simple, it is exposed. Finish the first half of the rehearsal singing this through—the first section from memory—and there is a communal sense of achievement of some expressive singing.

5. After a break, we turn to the *Sanctus*—the two-choir section needs intensive rehearsal. Spend time on vocal lines in small groupings, the two soprano parts, then the two alto parts. Put them together in varying grouping—the sopranos and the tenors, followed by the altos and the basses; then Choir 1 alone, then Choir 2 alone, and finally all together. All singers thus have the chance to hear how this fugal section is constructed and how their individual parts fit in and relate to the others. The pacing here has to be brisk and efficient, because singers have to be patient (and attentive) while they are not actually singing. All the time the tempo is varied according to the singers' needs and sung to "doo" as well as to the Latin text. Finally, all is put together, moved up to speed and energized. The rehearsal ends on a climax.

The principles and strategies outlined in this example can be transferred to other choral rehearsing contexts, whether the program consists of a variety of more straightforward individual pieces for young singers in school, or a major work like the *Requiem*. The next rehearsal would revise some of the work achieved in this one, as well as move on to new material.

VERBAL AND NON-VERBAL LANGUAGE

Following the idea of creating an appropriate learning environment in the choral rehearsal is the whole issue of effective communication. It has already been mentioned, borne out by Mehrabian's research, that only 10 percent of our communication is through verbal means. Talk, verbal explanation, and instruction clearly have their place in any communal and social situation, but conductors need to remember that music speaks louder than words, and body language and conducting gesture might communicate more efficiently and accurately what is required musically. One could equally say that the written word, such as appears in this very text, is a less effective method of conveying the nature of choral conducting than practical demonstration. Students constantly remind me that practical activity produces more learning than a string of words in written or oral form. The traditional lecture format is not an optimum way of learning—it just imparts information and stimulates thinking; but only further reading and, in our case, practical application will determine the level of real learning. Similarly, in the rehearsal situation, verbal instructions will have limited effect unless practical application follows. That is the craft skill of choral rehearsing and conducting.

How many times have we heard conductors talking excessively and giving too many verbal instructions all at once? In conducting classes, students often have a keen idea of what they want, technically and expressively, from the singers, and, after the first run-through of a piece, give a long list of verbal instructions. If I then ask the singers to recall that student conductor's verbal instructions, faces look blank: they cannot remember everything. Reinforcement of musical instructions will be more effective if delivered one by one and followed by practical application of the instruction or point made. Reinforcement will be even more effective if singers recognize the issues while singing and if the conductors can, through gesture, attend to problems as they occur. To give a simple example, a crescendo can be explained or felt. An exaggerated gesture with the conductor moving toward the singers to indicate something is about to happen will attract their attention and give them clues. The crescendo itself will not happen unless conductors indicate it in gesture regardless of the number of times it has been requested verbally. We will explore in the next chapter how singers can use gestures to help gain particular musical outcomes.

The use of imagery and analogy in the choral rehearsal can facilitate meaningful interpretation of musical character and be so much more effective than any technical instruction. Even with a talented group of singers, I employ imagery all the time. "Imagine singing this in a dark, gothic French cathedral with the smell of incense pervading the air . . . and let yourself float," I said to a high school choir when I was acting as a choral clinician during a festival. They were singing (and beautifully, too) Duruflé's motet *Ubi caritas*. They knew it well and were able to sing from memory. However, I wanted just a bit more of the still, hushed, and mystical atmosphere that should envelope its gentle exquisite harmonies. Even though most of the singers had not been to France, let alone sung in a French cathedral, they were able to visualize something of the image I had created and then moved a long way to capture the appropriate atmosphere. The music was transformed and became more than a performance of accurate notes. Asking young children, for example, to sing like a giant will create in their bodyminds a tonal concept that they are able to imagine and act upon. Think of sunshine, darkness, cold, trembling, fresh morning dew—all such words and images add color and character to the singers' imaginations that will more accurately portray the musical intention than a whole load of technical jargon, which often confuses.

A valuable example of the use (or non-use) of language comes from an experienced music teacher in an inner London primary (elementary) school working with a hall full of children. The beginning of this choral rehearsal just seemed to happen. She simply started warm-up exercises and vocalizes without any verbal instruction at all. The children, generally full of the joys of childhood and an urban environment, gradually settled and joined in the activity as they realized what was happening around them. The teacher carried on and swept the children along with her without any speaking. They instinctively knew what to do and what was expected of them. She was able to communicate everything, including certain musical nuances, through her gestures, eye contact, and general body language. The event was not fraught with instructions and reprimands, but rather dominated by musical activity. Conversely, I witnessed a very different situation in which a music teacher was rehearsing a group of secondary school boys for a small singing performance. She spent an unnecessary amount of time in verbal instruction, displayed no sense of fun or personal enjoyment of the music being rehearsed, and the musical outcome was dull and unconfident. While she showed signs of being perfectly competent and knowledgeable musically, there was no real communication with the boys that brought the music to life.

MOVEMENT IN THE CHORAL REHEARSAL

Some years ago on a bright summer's day, I decided to visit Ely Cathedral with a choral director friend. Ely is a small town just ten miles north of Cambridge in the East Anglian flat Fenland region of England. Dominating the town is a large, imposing, and beautiful cathedral. One of the cathedral's impressive features is its Lady Chapel, a lofty, light, and spacious chapel to the side of the main body of the cathedral, which has a wonderful, resonant acoustic. On this particular day, a primary school choir was rehearsing for its end-of-term concert or service in the Lady Chapel. We observed from the back of the chapel as serried ranks of young children were singing a rather unimpressive song, one of these popular idiom-type religious songs that are supposed to appeal to the masses but have little intrinsic musical worth. They were led by a brusque lady in a floral dress, who every now and then made somewhat jerking gestures toward the young singers with her arms. When the song came to an end, the first comment she made to the children, in a reprimanding tone, was "You must stand still when you sing!" My friend and I looked at each other, both of us wanting to scream, or at least take over the rehearsal from this teacher and "rescue" the young singers. But we gracefully withdrew. What she had unwittingly done was to deny the children what was for them a natural response to the music. They were able to capture something of the character of the song by the natural movement of their bodies. Also, more significantly, the teacher had implanted in their minds the notion that choral singing was to be associated with standing still. You do not move when singing; you should become tense and stiff when singing: these are the messages that the children could well have taken away with them, perhaps even associated with the way you sing in church. In addition to all that was the fact that the first comment she made to the children after their singing was a negative one—"you must . . . "—the language of control described in chapter 2. It would have been so easy to offer a comment of support or praise in the first instance that would have raised their morale and inspired them.

There is, nevertheless, a more significant issue concerning movement in the choral rehearsal that has been alluded to in previous chapters. First, I have already referred to physical preparation and warm-ups for the rehearsal: these can relieve tension and assist in mental preparation. Ideally such preparation would induce a freedom of bodily movement that would permeate the singers' bodyminds while making music. Second, there are specific movements or movement gestures that characterize and reflect music's aesthetic and expressive properties; these are kinesthetic actions and responses. Such movements and gestures employed by the singers help shape a musical phrase, for example, or gain insight into ways of effectively interpreting a musical passage or dealing technically with a particularly challenging musical extract. I am not referring in this context to forms of "choralography"—set dancelike movements or steps to music—however appropriate these might be in particular musical contexts like show and gospel choirs and singing spirituals, for example. The use of movement in the choral rehearsal is intended to be a rehearsal strategy, to help singers gain insight into the musical character of a piece by experiencing the music kinesthetically. By freeing the body from the usual rigid, stilted stance sometimes associated with formal choirs, singers will be able to gain in musical understanding—what we call the development of musicianship.

Let us return to the crescendo. Gesture for this needs to start low down within the frame of the body to ensure support for the vocal tone as well as indicate the increase in dynamics, rather a similar concept to the power in a swimming stroke coming from below the water's surface. This will have an even more profound effect if the singers are asked physically to imitate the conductor's gesture at this point. One example where this strategy could be effectively employed is toward the end of the *Benedictus* section of Haydn's *Nelson Mass*. The choir needs not only to sustain the dynamic but also the vocal tone in these bars.

If movement is closely associated with imagery and analogy, this will help the singers to understand the purpose of particular movement gestures. In the Haydn *Nelson Mass,* a useful image and kinesthetic connection is to ask the singers to imagine pushing a boulder up a hill, thus creating a resistance, yet steady momentum in the singing toward the inevitable climax. The purpose is to make the crescendo by creating a kinesthetic resistance in the singing, the physical act providing the musical understanding—the bodymind connection. The imagery is helpful, but the physical movement associated with pushing the boulder up the hill even more effectively connects the musical outcome with the feelings and sensations encountered. By imagining and feeling the resistance of a boulder being pushed up a hill, the singers are able to feel the resistance of a steady crescendo through the musical phrase. That image will become internalized in the bodymind and easily recalled during the performance of that passage. A simple cue as, for example, writing the word "boulder" in the score or some iconic indication will trigger the internalized memory feeling of the crescendo. Note also how Haydn cleverly crafts the climax with the use of the repeated triplet figure in the orchestra to contrast with and complement the vocal writing.

Other useful movements or gestures that can be incorporated into the choral rehearsal might include shaping a legato musical phrase with a sweeping arm gesture, bending the knees and feeling kinesthetically a lifting of a phrase, for example. Another might be a pointing or jabbing movement to gain a staccato feeling to a musical passage. (Some of these will be explored further in chapter 8 on gesture.) All these can be useful tools in rehearsals that will be internalized for concert performance. But most important, singers should be allowed to respond naturally and physically to music. The instruction to "stand still" has mental associations of rigidity, tension, and consequently inefficient singing.

I observed one young conductor using a variety of gestures with her high school madrigal choir to try to sort out a tuning problem. The piece was an arrangement for the King's Singers of *You are the New Day,* and the baritones were having difficulty in pitching a particular note accurately in a chord. In order to deal with the situation, she asked them to copy her with a "spiraling" gesture, followed by a "climbing a ladder" movement with their hands. However, at no time did she verbally reprimand them for their tuning difficulty; rather, she tried to deal with it without drawing it to their attention unnecessarily. She took responsibility for the problem, sharing it with them rather than blaming them. How often do we see conductors blaming their singers for a problem and passing the responsibility on to them without giving any help? Not only did the problem in this case eventually diminish, but also the young singers themselves were enabled to solve the problem without losing face. An effective method of communication was in evidence; the conductor clearly had a good rapport with the young singers as rehearsals were held each morning at 7 o'clock! Throughout this particular early morning rehearsal, she maintained good communication through her gesture and body language as well as by verbal means to create an appropriate learning environment for the young singers. Learning had taken place. The singers left the rehearsal in an exuberant and confident manner—presumably (as I did) to have breakfast!

Movement and gesture then can contribute to musical understanding. As we know, dance and movement in certain cultures is so integral to music that there is no separate word in the language to distinguish the two. I have consistently found a freedom in vocal sound when conductors have encouraged their singers to adopt a relaxed posture. I often ask my singers to concentrate on their ankles—yes, ankles—and create for themselves a freedom of motion and flexibility from the ankles by moving from the ankle joints. The knees then automatically become unlocked and the whole lower torso to the hips will generate a tension-free condition that in turn will bring about tension-free singing. A reminder to the choir to maintain flexible ankles can be helpful to gain fluidity when singing particular legato musical phrases. This also somehow prevents harsh vocal timbres. The bodymind connection equates a stiff, rigid posture with stiff, rigid singing, and flexible, malleable posture will be more likely to stimulate gentle, released singing.

SPACING AND ACOUSTICS

Sound, as an acoustical phenomenon, is a complex area. It concerns not only the physics of space, but also interesting pedagogical dimensions if applied to spacing of a choir in a choral rehearsal. There are a number of individual sound sources that make up the composite sound of a choir. Exploration of and experimentation with the spacing of singers in rehearsal situations can have many positive outcomes, not only on the quality of the choral sound, but also on the musical learning skills of the singers and their self-perceptions.

Often regular choir rehearsals take place in a different venue from the concerts. Some of the problems associated with final rehearsals in concert venues occur because of the singers' adjustment to the acoustics and the perception of a "new" sound. Suddenly standing next to someone singing a different vocal part in a final rehearsal can be an unnerving experience, especially if the resonance of the building contrasts with the normal rehearsal room. If singers remain in the same place in each rehearsal, new venues and placings may well cause problems. Some people feel threatened in unfamiliar surroundings and therefore will not be able to perform as easily and without tension. If singers feel alone in new surroundings, they are unlikely to be able to give their best. Conductors would be well advised to encourage flexibility among their singers with regard to their position in the choir: get them used to hearing different voices around them.

James Daugherty has researched extensively the physical, pedagogical, and philosophical dimensions of choir spacing and choral sound.[6] From my own experience, I have found that singers, when fairly confident about their own vocal part, are usually aware of the benefits to the choral sound of, for example, a mixed-voice formation. Daugherty goes further to explore how spacing—particularly the distance between individual singers—influences choral sound. He reports that singers who took part in his research consistently and significantly preferred "spread" spacing over "close" spacing. The benefits included more independent singing, improved vocal production, and the ability to hear the ensemble and one's own voice more effectively. Clearly there are problems with space in a small room with a large choir, but even so, the physical dimension of singers' placement and spacing ought to be explored and consideration given to the choral sound in the various formations wherever possible.

Singers can gain much confidence and self-esteem when they feel they contribute to the overall sound independently. They become less reliant on fellow singers and also are more likely to listen to the overall sound and become increasingly aware of tuning. Often, inaccurate tuning is passed from voice to voice in a section of the choir. If the tuning is less secure, then one by one singers drag each other down in pitch, as each hears what they believe to be the appropriate pitch. A pitch-unconfident soprano singing next to another pitch-unconfident soprano, singing next to a loud and not always pitch-accurate soprano, will have a disastrous effect on the whole soprano section. In contrast, a soprano singing next to an alto is more likely to assist the overall pitch accuracy because she is hearing supporting harmony. Of course, it is not a good idea with an amateur choir of less experienced or less confident singers to begin learning a piece in this mixed-voice formation because this may well reduce confidence and self-esteem if singers feel threatened. However, once a piece of music has been learned, or even by using a well-known song, it is worth spacing the choir in a more spread formation and letting the singers appreciate any difference in the sound.

Finally, there are musical considerations with regard to choir spacing. Throughout history, choirs have sung in a variety of spacings, formations, and acoustics. We have the *cori spezzati* of Renaissance Venice responding to the demands of the acoustics of St. Mark's Cathedral, reflected in the music of the Gabriellis, Monteverdi, and Schutz, for example. Here two choirs would sing from opposite sides of the cathedral in sacred music that was composed in antiphonal style.

In many cathedrals today in England, the choir assumes an inward-facing position on either side of a central aisle, each side with its full complement of voice parts, thus assuming to be two choirs of equal voices. The psalms of the day are often sung antiphonally on a regular basis: verse by verse, choir by choir.

Formation of Typical Cathedral or Church Choir in England			
B	S	S	B
B	S	S	B
T	S	S	T
T	S	S	T
A	S	S	A
A	S	S	A
	Conductor		

The performance of much English as well as Italian Renaissance music would be improved by this positioning, as in, for example, the eight-part setting of *O Clap Your Hands* by Orlando Gibbons, which has distinctive antiphonal sections within the anthem. Sopranos, altos, tenors, and basses of Choir 1 are positioned on one side and those of Choir 2 on the other. Whenever such two-choir antiphonal style of music is rehearsed even with a larger choir, it is a good idea to position singers so that they can appreciate the intended effect as fully as possible. Generally in polyphonic music, it may well be advantageous to have the voice parts in sections in order that the polyphony might be heard clearly.

More common with choirs performing in concert halls is the straight-line formation, normally with voice parts in section blocks.

Sopranos   Altos   Tenors   Basses

or

Sopranos   Tenors   Basses   Altos

Where possible and where for musical reasons it is necessary to keep parts reasonably in blocks, and when the sopranos and altos outnumber the tenors and basses, it might be desirable to position the tenors and basses centrally.

Alto 1   Soprano 1   Tenors   Basses   Soprano 2   Alto 2

There is considerable advantage to adopting a mixed formation in choirs when singing homophonic music, for example. A formation that consists of a series of groups of SATB (either four or eight voices depending on the size of the full choir) could well promote a more ideal, homogenous blend of voices in the overall choral sound. The following plan might well be an ideal one for an experienced and confident choir of 32 with an equal number of voices in each part. It will require judicious placing of voices in order to establish a satisfactory choral blend. This exercise in itself can be an interesting one to hear how voices can match and blend quite differently in various positions.

[Several mixed formations of sopranos, altos, tenors and basses depending on numbers in each part]			
S A S A	T B S A	S B S B	S A T B
T B T B	S A T B	A T T A	S A T B

However, in reality most choirs will not have equal numbers of voices in each part. It may well be that a choir will have up to twice as many sopranos and altos as tenors and basses. Of course, it is often desirable to have more sopranos and basses than altos and tenors, but that depends on strength of voices, acoustics, and the repertoire being performed. Depending on the strength of individual voices this again will need careful experiment and adjustment. Involving the singers themselves in making these decisions can enhance the entire learning and performing experience.

Wouldn't it be really exciting if occasionally we could abandon the conventional formal positioning of choirs for concerts and explore a more dynamic and varying soundscape? What about surrounding the audience with sound? What about processing into the hall or church singing, or even inviting the audience to participate in some capacity? It is all about getting the singers accustomed to varying formations and spacings with the result that they will become increasingly confident in their own singing, and, who knows, the conductor may even become less intrusive and controlling!

INTELLIGENT REHEARSING

Rehearsing singers requires a degree of social intelligence, an awareness of what is happening in the group both musically and socially. Combined with planning and knowing what to cover in a particular rehearsal period, social intelligence offers strategies for dealing with musical issues in what can often be a sensitive situation. What we are dealing with is people, their emotional and spiritual lives as well as the musical issues. This demands intelligence or perhaps a series of intelligences (as suggested by the psychologist Howard Gardner). Gardner identifies music as a distinct intelligence—a right-side brain phenomenon (see chapter 2)—but also identifies other capability-ability clusters that are required by the successful and effective conductor: interpersonal skills is one of these, as is communicating with and motivating people in the singing activity.[7] Emotional intelligence has already been referred to, and is something expressive conductors need to elicit expressive and meaningful singing from the choir collectively as well as individually. I suggest that there is a range of intelligences or capability-ability clusters beyond Gardner's multiple ones that come into play for the choral conductor in various situations.

When asking undergraduate students to keep a journal and review of rehearsals they attended over a semester, I was surprised at their acute perception of what they consider makes for an effective and not-so-effective rehearsal and how the conductors' various intelligences come into play (or not as the case may be). Here are some of their comments taken from a variety of rehearsals with different conductors of instrumental as well as choral ensembles:

- The conductor kept the energy high in the choir, especially when he smiled if it sounded good. . . . He reminded the singers of the progress they made last time and stated what his plan was for the piece in this rehearsal. . . . He asked the singers to caress the "important words," but he didn't tell them what the important words were. This was a good way of letting the singers feel in control and letting them show what they know.
- One point we focused on in class was being in control of a rehearsal—but how much control is *too* much control? Personally, I felt that at times Conductor A's control of the ensemble went a little too far and began to intimidate the players. This subsequently had its repercussions in both rehearsal and performance.
- Here is what a rehearsal consists of: tuning, running the piece completely through (bear in mind that this is not the first time the piece has been worked on, read, or in some cases performed), stopping and *talking* [student's italics] about what was good, bad, needed to be worked on, etc. He would then lapse into some old story, which would probably lead into another . . .
- He worked the musicians hard [yes, this reference is to singers, which is welcome] and got good results because of his energy and encouragement. . . . Another aspect of the rehearsal that the conductor handled well was time management. He was very efficient, and it was clear that he had thought hard about what he wanted to accomplish during the rehearsal.
- The pacing of the rehearsal was good—he kept things moving so the students didn't get bored. He was very inclusive in his choice of language saying "let's do this," etc. This conductor gave lots of

positive feedback and constructive criticism. A really nice thing he did was thanking them for a good rehearsal at the end so they know that he appreciated their efforts.

- I liked a lot of the musical suggestions and he made a few good points. However, when he pointed out the parts that needed improvement, it was done negatively. It wasn't that what he said was bad, just how he said it, and that made all the difference in how the ensemble responded. The pace of the rehearsal was very slow and the students seemed to get bored quickly. This made them lose focus and reduced the quality of the sound. Overall the group had a nice blend, but seemed to be glad when the rehearsal was over.
- It's the morale of the group that I worry about with this conductor. It almost seemed like he picked out spots before the rehearsal to criticize before even hearing them played. On a couple of instances the ensemble sounded fine, but the conductor would stop the group and drill a point about a section that did not seem to be an issue. . . . This conductor gets the job done but at the cost of an inspired ensemble.
- The conductor displayed a lot of energy and love for the music through his dancelike movements while conducting. . . . The conductor did not hold back his praise and presented his criticisms in a motivational manner. This makes all the difference for a musician.

It is evident from these journal entries that students do not want to be reprimanded (and I suspect the same could be said of anyone being conducted). Similarly every mistake does not need to be pointed out. Allowing singers to take target practice and make their own adjustments as far as possible will enable them to feel good about themselves by gaining mastery of skills and thus enhancing self-esteem (see chapter 2). Criticism in a "motivational manner," as one student wrote, is a rather nice phrase that captures the essence of part of the conductors' role in rehearsals. This kind of approach will more likely enhance the morale of the ensemble, as will the use of inviting, "inclusive" language. The message essentially is that singers and instrumentalists actually *want* to get better at what they do; they want to achieve musically. The very fact that they belong to a musical ensemble means that they need that sense of belonging and togetherness that making music encapsulates and fosters. What they don't need is to be made to feel inadequate. Rehearsing is making music; it is not just a means to an end, a preparation for something that is more important. Avoid the notion of trying not to get it *wrong*, but rather keep taking target practice at the bull's-eye.

8

LESS IS MORE: CONDUCTING GESTURE

A flautist student of mine was playing in an orchestra. She had several measures' rest and was anticipating her next entry. As the moment approached, the conductor looked toward her and held up his hand with the palm facing her. She had a very quick panic: what was she to do? Did he mean "stop," or was this some absurd way of indicating her entry? Within a split second she made the decision to continue and play the flute entry as indicated in the score. Her panic was clearly an unnecessary predicament, and she continued to feel uneasy for the rest of the performance. The conductor's gesture on this occasion was ambiguous and might as easily have been interpreted as "don't come in—stop." The gesture was open to misinterpretation. The conductor, it would seem, had not really studied the nature of communication through gesture nor understood the import of particular gestures and signals.

This is an extreme example of ambiguous gesture and one that is, I would like to believe, rare in conducting situations. However, I do believe that conductors need to develop a gesture vocabulary that will unambiguously inform, indicate, and suggest a whole range of musical responses from the singers and players they conduct. While gesture and non-verbal communication is a theme that permeates this text, this chapter will explore in particular conducting gesture and its impact and influence on singers and the music that they produce. For conducting to be effective, gesture in all its contours matters more than verbal language. In concert performance, of course, verbal language becomes redundant, and gesture is everything.

GESTURE AND COMMUNICATION

It is key to an aesthetic activity like making music that we move away from excessive verbalizing. Conducting gestures throughout the ages have had different purposes—from beating time in the Sistine Chapel to the expressive forms that many conductors adopt today (see chapter 4). The conductor was not really considered an interpreter of music until the nineteenth century, when large orchestral and choral forces and increasing demands of composers in terms of rubato phrasing, flexible tempi, and rhythmic complexity made the conductor a significant figure. The musical pedagogy of Dalcroze and Kodály are examples of other styles of gestural communication that have also been used with group music making to indicate, for example, specified pitches.

How we respond to gesture is, of course, a most interesting subject of study. We know that certain hand gestures, for example, have different meanings depending on which part of the world you live in. Desmond Morris, author and psychologist, made a fascinating research study of the meaning of gestures through western and southern Europe.[1] His research team explored the origins and distribution of emblematic or symbolic gestures (that is, those that are not natural additions to the spoken dialogue). They found a number of common meanings in gestures, but also marked differences from country to country, culture to culture, and even region to region. The common thumbs-up gesture, for example, indicates "OK" extensively throughout Europe, though in southern Sardinia, Sicily, and parts of Greece it is regarded as a sexual insult.

Gestures themselves can mean more than defined words: they have connotations. A person's anger can be verbalized, but shown much more strongly through gesture—a banging or shaking of the fist. Together with facial expressions and other non-verbal communications, the meaning and intention becomes stronger. Gesture is often more informative than words to indicate changing moods and emotional states, certainly in our business of artistic activity. Just walk around where you work or at home and notice how people gesture and how significant such gesture is to the intent of the communication. I know I use hand gestures a lot in conversation, and several people have asked me if I am able to talk without using my hands. "I am a conductor," I respond. If, for example, I describe the view from a hilltop, as I did on a snow-capped hill in Wales last New Year's Day, I use my hands and arms to outline the space in front of me. "Just look … " needs a gesture. Also, if I am describing my favorite Hockney painting to someone, I am shaping certain elements or components of the picture, be it a person, swimming pool, or other object. This will occur even if I am looking at the painting with someone.

Just look at how people in an art gallery talk or describe to their companions. And, of course, look at the importance of gesture for the hearing impaired, who rely on its literal and connotative meanings. Sometimes I wonder if on certain occasions we need words at all.

MUSICAL GESTURES

There are two essential ingredients to a conductor's gestures. One is concerned with the more "literal," giving a signal type of gesture: beating time, keeping pulse, and, perhaps to a lesser extent, indicating entries. The other is the "connotative" gesture that helps to create the expressive character of the music, by following the musical phrase and providing the musical meaning. There are accepted and well-practiced beat patterns that tell the conducted where they are in the score. The patterns are particularly important for instrumental players who often have to count bars of rest. In music that is complex rhythmically or with changing meter, members of the ensemble certainly need to know when the first beat of each bar occurs. Orchestral players performing Walton's *Belshazzar's Feast* or the *Symphony of Psalms* by Stravinsky will unquestionably need conductors to provide clear indications through commonly accepted conducting patterns of where the beats are, in what are often varied meters and tempi in these twentieth-century choral works.

Accompanied recitatives in baroque opera and oratorio are examples of situations in which, because there may be some flexibility in the solo singer's tempo, the unambiguous indication of the first beat in each particular bar and punctuating chords at the cadences are vital. Let's look at the well-known series of recitatives from Handel's *Messiah* (you will find it useful to refer to your own score at this point):

> There were shepherds . . .
> And lo, the angel of the Lord . . .
> And the angel said unto them . . .
> And suddenly there was with the angel . . .

These recitatives follow in quick succession, as they have the role of announcing to the shepherds the birth of Jesus Christ. The first and third are *secco* recitatives played only by continuo instruments. The conductor here will need to indicate clearly the chord changes. In order to make the music sound fluent, it is vital to follow the text, feeling the movement of the phrase that is triggered by the text. The conductor will anticipate the phrase, thus preparing the chord change. The beat will not necessarily be strict in tempo, but rather will be governed by the movement and meaning of the text. In contrast, the second and fourth recitatives are *accompagnato* with the orchestra playing. The nature of the accompaniment suggests a less flexible approach to the tempo in order to accommodate in this instance the arpeggio semiquavers (sixteenth notes) played by the violins. The conductor will need to provide a clear and even "four-in-a-bar" pattern.

I do not intend to supply a textbook coverage of conducting patterns—these can be found elsewhere—except to point out that there is a customary pattern of beating two, three, and four, which beginning conductors need to establish firmly in order to be able to move beyond and within those established patterns. Conducting is a craft skill that requires practice: conducting recitatives even more so. I often use these for conducting classes, as they provide students with the chance to follow the soloists and the text, deal with flexibility within a tempo, and give clear unambiguous cadences at the ends of phrases and starts to new ones. Because of the nature of recitatives—they carry the bulk of the story line in the text and therefore have important narrative—the movement of the musical phrases should be determined by the words of the text. In the third of these four recitatives there is a lot of important text:

And the **an**gel said unto |them, "|**Fear** not: for be|hold, I bring you good |**tid**ings of great **joy,** which shall |be to all **peo**ple. For unto **you** is born this |**day,** in the city of |**David,** A **Saviour,** which is |**Christ** the **Lord.**"

I have made bold what I believe to be significant words in the lyrical musical context. Moving the phrase toward these words ensures the movement and fluidity of the whole recitative. The conducting gesture will reflect this by being a little more emphatic on the bold words and syllables, even though they may not always appear on the first beat of the bar. By moving the phrase forward, the excitement of the text—in this case the angel's announcement of the birth of Christ—will be captured and also anticipate the frenzy of the following recitative and its buildup to the dynamic of the chorus "*Glory to God.*" It will not be necessary or appropriate to conduct a pattern that gives equal emphasis to each beat, or even, in this instance, to make an emphatic first beat of each bar if the words do not suggest an emphasis.

Too many conductors plod through a four-beat pattern accommodating no difference in the style, magnitude, or shape of gesture whether they are conducting an intimate motet or a boisterous march. This is often the case with conductors of children's groups or amateur ensembles. Perhaps it is perceived as a way of keeping control or perhaps the conductor does not sufficiently trust the performers. Rigid, unchanging, and exaggerated beat patterns add little to the aesthetic dimension of music. And young children are just as capable as any professional group of responding to small, expressive gestures: let them.

The point of each beat—the *ictus*—can indicate a pointed "attack" or a "release" of the sound. Both indicate the moment of sound, but each style of gesture can determine the particular quality of the sound. Let us look at the first bars of the chorus *Glory to God* that follows those four recitatives.

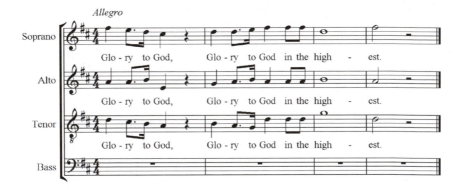

Imagine the quality of the sound, with the bright timbre of trumpets and drums accompanying the chorus (not included in this extract). What sort of sound do we want from the choir at their entry on "Glory"? It most probably needs a sound that complements the sound of the orchestra: a bright, clear, dynamic sound. Whatever timbral quality is required, this will be a sound—especially with the consonant "Gl"—that needs preparation by the singers and so by the conductor. Try singing "Glo . . . " and think of the position of the mouth and tongue in particular before the sound actually is produced. There is quite a lot of energy required to get the sound out. The conductor will therefore need to provide a release in the gesture that allows the sound to move toward the vowel "o." A sharp attacking gesture may work for the trumpets, but the singers will more ideally require the gesture to simulate the release of the sound. Also they will ideally require a facial expression from the conductor that will enable them to create an appropriate shape and vowel sound. That is not to say that conductors should mouth the words, because in certain pieces and situations this can give misleading messages to the singers. But the conductor can help by emulating the shape for the "Glo . . . "

Preparation for and release of the choral sound is very much embodied in the conductors' gesture. It is interesting for conductors themselves to explore this with their choirs. Try conducting the opening chord of any piece, a well-known song, for example, with two contrasting gestures— one attacking and the other releasing—and ask the choir if they can recognize a difference in the sound they produced. Do *you* notice a difference? Allowing the choir to be aware of the difference in sound a conducting gesture can generate will enable them to understand that conducting is more than keeping time. (It may even prompt them to look at us more!) The opening choral chord of the *Hallelujah* from *Messiah* might be an example where an attacking gesture will generate a glottal hard "Ahh" whereas a more releasing gesture will generate a less hard sound—more of a "Hahh." Either can be appropriate for the music; I give the example just to illustrate the possibilities and contrasts. Gesture makes a difference.

An interesting experiment I often carry out with beginning conducting students is to ask them to sing something well known to them and conduct it simultaneously. (I usually suggest *My Country 'Tis of Thee* or *God Save the Queen* depending on nationality—but any known song will do.) I then ask them to sing the same thing in a marcato style, but conduct it in a legato style and vice versa. They invariably find this difficult. The bodymind is receiving contradictory messages and cannot process either the marcato or the legato very successfully. Another experiment is to conduct the song with big, extravagant gestures but sing very quietly: again, mixed messages are received. If a conductor consistently gives out misleading signals in this way, then gradually the singers will cease to attend either to verbal or gestural instructions.

Gesture to attack sound.

I recall watching a conductor rehearsing with choir and orchestra who seemed frustrated with the balance of sound between the two groups and asked the orchestra to play quietly. However, his gesture was very large and sweeping and continued in that style in spite of the instruction, so much so that it was really difficult for the players to play quietly. He was

Gesture to release sound.

giving a mixed message: on the one hand his gesture suggested broad loud playing whereas on the other the verbal instruction was to play quietly. Conducting gesture is much more than beating time. It needs to be unambiguous and support the conductor's goals.

TWO OR FOUR? ... AND MORE

Let's now look at Mozart's well-known and exquisite motet *Ave verum corpus* to explore some further aspects of conducting gesture. I believe that this motet can be performed effectively in a variety of tempi. The chosen tempo should ideally depend on the acoustics of the performance venue as well as the size and experience of the choir. I have performed it very slowly—a real adagio—as well as in a more lilting andantino tempo.

The matter of conducting four or two in a bar needs consideration. Ideally at whatever tempo it is taken, the feeling of two in the bar will promote a fuller sense of phrasing and breathing rather than a more plodding four. Nevertheless, there are moments during the motet when conducting "four in a bar" is appropriate. It may be a good idea to start the piece in four for the accompaniment, and it will certainly be appropriate to use four when a slight pulling back of the tempo is applied at the end of particular phrases and especially at the end on the word "examine." A two-in-a-bar pattern in a slow tempo needs control, a feeling of resistance through the movement in the air. The final section on the words "esto nobis" particularly needs the feeling of resistance building up to its climax; the conducting gesture will not only provide the two-in-a-bar pattern, but do so with an open supporting gesture to ensure strength of vocal tone during a crescendo.

The supporting gesture will normally involve the palm of the hand facing upward and kept low in line with the conductor's abdominal area; this reflects the support needed in singers' breathing from their abdominal areas. A gesture like this is more likely to promote supported musical phrases and supported tone than verbal instruction alone. Even more effective would be to encourage the singers themselves to use this gesture when rehearsing, so that they can internalize the feeling of vocal support during this particular passage. Just get them to imitate the supportive gesture with one or both hands themselves and let them feel and recognize any difference in the tone quality. (Recall the example cited in chapter 7 with regard to the *Benedictus* from Haydn's *Nelson Mass* and the image of pushing the boulder up a hill.)

Another contrasting example to consider is the arrangement by William Dawson of the spiritual *Ev'ry Time I Feel the Spirit*. As with the Mozart motet, there are four beats in a bar. While it indeed is in

Supporting conducting gesture.

a brisk tempo, there are advantages to conducting a neat, tight four in a bar pattern at the beginning following the first two pause (fermata) chords in order to establish a rhythmic vitality to the singing. However, once established, the piece hardly needs conducting until the final bars, when the pause (fermata) chords and the molto allargando can be really pulled back and each chord separated at the conductor's discretion.

The conductor's main role in this piece is to maintain its vitality through facial expression and neat pointed gesture in the beat to emphasize the syncopation. Syncopation itself never needs to be conducted; the "on" beats must be maintained in order that singers feel the offbeat rhythms. Here conductors should encourage singers to feel the music by "allowing" them to move freely while singing. It simply does not look appropriate to have singers standing poker still while performing music like this. Conductors themselves might ideally also adopt a freedom of movement, rather than become absorbed with conducting patterns. This will more readily reflect the required musical expression and character.

Bob Chilcott's *Irish Blessing* is a beautiful setting of some beautiful words. As with the previous two pieces described, a four-in-a-bar conducting pattern might be appropriate at the beginning to establish the flowing movement of the piano accompaniment. However, when the voices enter on the words "May the road rise to meet you," the character of that phrase will be more adequately reflected by moving into two—feeling the "road rising"—with a resistance in the gesture similar to that described in relation to Mozart's *Ave verum corpus*. The four beats can be employed more judiciously when certain phrase endings slow down, for example, when the tempo altogether slows toward the end. The gesture will need to reflect the words; they are gentle, reflective words of well-wishing and longing, and conductors will need to provide little more than a gentle, reflective gesture to shape the phrases and the text rather than beat time.

These three musical examples illustrate that four in a bar is not just for fast music and two in a bar just for slow: that is far too simplistic. My point is that the music itself tells the conductor how to conduct. By understanding and adopting an essentially kinesthetic response to the music's expressive character, conductors will become efficient and expressive.

Conductors do not need to control by excessive time beating or exaggerated gesture, rather they need to allow the music's character to come through by suggesting and largely keeping the conducting gestures within the body's frame. Wild, extravagant gestures in these examples are simply not necessary, whether you are conducting a professional choir or a choir of less experienced young people. Gestures should be an aesthetic reflection of the character of the music, and they are intended to be more of a cue and indication to singers than a controlling mechanism. Conducting gestures are a kinesthetic embodiment of music and an enabling procedure for singers. They are kinesthetic symbolic modes of expression, as music itself is a symbolic mode of human expression. Conducting gestures need not be exhaustive (or exhausting), nor should they do everything for singers. Trusting singers is part of a key strategy for promoting effective learning and singing and giving them ownership of the musical experience. If conductors trust their singers, then they do not need to control them by gesture, rather they remind them. Less is more.

Ideally, those intending to become choral conductors, or those who already are, will reflect on their own practices and develop their own gesture vocabulary. Professional dialogue and professional development should include opportunities to conduct in front of other conductors and experiment and explore gestures in rehearsals with singers. There is no need to become defensive about conducting: be open to comment and seek out ways to develop more meaningful gestures.

HELPFUL GESTURES

Alongside literal gestures (those that give us the pulse and sense of where we are in musical direction) and connotative gestures (those that suggest the expressive character and nuance of the music) we have other styles of gestures that are helpful in some technical or musical way. We have already referred to the supporting gesture that will enable the singers to breathe and sustain phrases: the upturned palm low in the abdominal region. It is not so easy to sing with short clavicular breathing when the gesture is low and open. Another useful gesture to help with intonation is the lifting of the palm as if gently pulling a puppet string (see photo).

I have found that this is immensely beneficial when exploring ways of improving intonation and lightening the vocal timbre, especially, but not exclusively, for some reason, with female voices. The importance of this particular gesture is that the raising of the inside of the palm reflects the raising of the soft palate, which is situated inside the mouth at the rear, which in turn will assist with tuning certain musical phrases or notes. The soft palate determines vocal resonance and overall tone quality and, consequently, the awareness of the raising of the soft palate will help to place and color vocal tone and often intonation. It is associated with the "sigh" and yawn, which themselves create a resonance. Get them to do it with you. So, again a bodymind connection is made, and if singers can rehearse with this gesture at the appropriate moments, they

Gesture to help raise the soft palette.

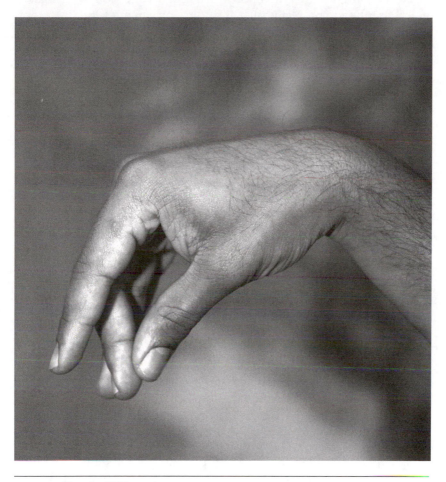

Close up of lifting gesture.

will internalize this for performance. The conductor can use it during rehearsal and performance to remind singers: it works.

Difficulties with tuning occur for a variety of reasons; it may be the acoustics of the room, the positioning of particular singers, or the perception of the music's harmonic structure, so conductors need to be open to exploration in order to deal with these difficulties (see chapter 7). Clearly, vocal production may need to be sorted out, and this is why the lifting gesture can go some way to enabling the singers: It is a vocally friendly gesture. Maybe this is all a psychological exercise, but sometimes, focusing too much on a problem makes it worse. We are then *trying* too hard, and that can often be a negative condition. Drawing too much attention to problems such as intonation can put a lot of stress on singers and consequently the vocal mechanism—then you get nowhere. I have often drawn attention away from a problem in rehearsals by asking singers to concentrate on something else, even their feet, for example; while perhaps not being a foolproof rehearsal strategy, it usually goes some way toward helping to solve the problem.

Other gestures that can be effective in the rehearsal context include ones that can be shared with the singers. Conducting with a "flicking" gesture imitated by the singers will create a lightness of tone; using more of a "stabbing" gesture will create a more marcato, stabbing sound; and so on. The imagery of stroking a cat (a good one for cat lovers), by actually stroking the back of the hand, can create a soft legato in the vocal sound, as singers will be able to visualize not only the stroking of the cat, but also the calm tenderness associated with that gesture. These gestures can be rehearsal ploys when used with the singers, but they can help to re-create that desired effect when the conductor uses them in performance. Visual gesture can conjure up from the mind that particular musical quality that has been rehearsed; the singers then can put it into action. It works: the bodymind connection again.

OPENING UP

During one open conducting seminar I was leading, I asked one of the student conductors if she would try to lower her whole conducting gesture because her arms were constantly raised high. I noticed that with a high gestural plane, her shoulders were rather hunched, and she seemed tense around the neck and shoulder area. This in time was reflected in the singers at the seminar; they too seemed to have raised shoulders, which in turn restricted the vocal tract and then the vocal tone. She was nevertheless very reluctant to change and stated emphatically that she had been conducting like this for 21 years and her choir seemed to be fine! What she did not understand was the argument that her choir might get even better if she adopted a lower and more relaxed conducting posture; they might themselves over time then develop a more relaxed and fuller vocal tone.

We sometimes get so used to and accepting of the sound of our choirs that we work with regularly, that we are not always aware of potential improvements that could be made in their vocal tone. And, by the way, I do know about the argument that "they can't see if I don't raise my arms," but another solution should be sought if this affects the quality of the singing.

The tables were turned one day in a graduate conducting class where I was demonstrating conducting a section of Fauré's *Cantique de Jean Racine*. At a certain subito p—the one where the sopranos sing a high G flat—a student pointed out that my gesture at that moment, while indicating the change in dynamic, was not helpful to her vocally, as it suggested a tightening and tensing of the vocal tract. Rather than become defensive about the situation, I encouraged the class to explore together a range of gestures in order to find the optimum one for that musical moment. Think about it for a moment: What do conductors do at a subito p? We tend to hunch our shoulders and shrink our necks and perhaps bring our conducting arms into our bodies. And what facial expressions do we give? Some of these gestures and body and facial expressions may not help the singer vocally. After all, what is the purpose of conducting gestures if they are not helpful to the singers? The most important outcome was that, from then on, I considered my gesture at that point in the *Cantique* and, I hope, in further performances provided a more vocal-friendly one to bring the singers' attention to and help shape the subito p. Although this may be considered to be minutiae and high-level conducting detail, the principle is that we should examine our gestures and ourselves and not be afraid to do so. Videotaping is an excellent way from time to time for carrying out a reality check on our conducting. What do our singers really see?

In conclusion, conducting gestures are effective if they are

- an aesthetic reflection and representation of musical expression
- efficient and unambiguous
- vocally friendly

Conductors themselves will become more effective if they are open to comment and adjustment.

As at the end of chapter 7 on rehearsing, I share with you some of the journal entries of students in my undergraduate conducting classes. Some of the comments on conducting gesture are also very perceptive. As before, they are of various conductors, and the comments are critical and both positive and negative:

- The biggest criticism of this conductor's style is that it is almost completely unvaried. I didn't sense any direction in the musical lines, and perhaps some direction and shaping shown by the conductor would have helped. Here is a perfect example of a conductor who looks angry and aggressive during the most beautiful music and then wonders why it isn't beautiful.

- Great facial expressions! Breathing is very good, helps keep the group together. His gestures are very fluid and moving but they tend to be on the large side.
- To go along with this conductor's dry, unproductive and seemingly endless rehearsals was a monotonous and somewhat mesmerizing conducting style. His conducting was stiff, rigid and very metronomic. I felt as though he was only there because he was being paid and not to create music.

These journal entries indicate that singers, players, and observers *do* know when conductors are expressive and clear, and are quite aware when they are not really committed to the music. We should not underestimate the perceptions of those we conduct. They are turned off by aggressive and demanding behavior from their conductors and by lack of clarity or inexpressive "metronomic" gestures. They are engaged by fluid, beautiful gestures that relate to the aesthetic dimension of the music.

I have referred in this chapter to "resistance" in gesture when discussing particular musical moments.[2] One very useful experience for me was to take a tai-chi class in a swimming pool. Here I really understood the notion of controlled resistance through space. Movement in water can be very graceful, and, when on dry land, imagined resistance of the water is an image that will provoke graceful conducting. I keep thinking I should hold some of my conducting classes in a pool!

Gesture is about communicating the essence of the music, not detracting from it. Inappropriate gestures—those that do not reflect the essence of the music—can impede musical progress, whereas appropriate ones enhance musical progress. In the rehearsal context, appropriate gestures fix the desirable expressive and vocal qualities of the music into the bodyminds of the singers, so that they will, responding to the gestural cue of the conductor in performance, be able to re-create the feelings encountered in rehearsals. Conducting gestures are the symbolic visual embodiment of music's character and need to support its full realization.

9

CONDUCTING AND VOCAL
DEVELOPMENT AND HEALTH

Throughout this book I have advocated that conductors can influence their singers in more ways than they might realize. We have looked at the way teachers and conductors can provide human-compatible and human-antagonistic learning situations. We have explored the way language and non-verbal communication, including conducting gestures, contribute to intended musical outcomes, especially in terms of vocal timbres and expressive singing. We have also considered aspects of rehearsing, attending to the principles and strategies that provide an appropriate learning environment for creating and feeling safe in the singing context. I would now like to attend to some aspects of vocal development and vocal health from the conducting perspective, areas that I believe conductors can influence, for good or for bad, by their verbal language and gestures.

For example, by gaining understanding of vocal development during adolescence, conductors and teachers will be more informed when making decisions and choices concerning repertoire. It will not be much use choosing inappropriate pieces for particular voice types and ages, as this will merely confirm a feeling of inadequacy in the singers. However much conductors have a passion for Mozart's *Requiem*, it will not be a suitable choice for very young children either in terms of the musical and vocal challenges or indeed handling the text. OK, so that is rather an extreme example, but the principle still applies.

EARLY YEARS SINGING DEVELOPMENT

Teachers working with young children probably avoid using the word "conductor" to describe themselves or "conducting" to describe the activity they are engaged in. But I would like to extend the definition of "conducting" to be inclusive of all those who lead singing and choral activities in their schools or communities. Conducting embraces teaching, leading, encouraging, motivating, and communicating. In the context of schools and young developing singers, conducting involves rehearsing, demonstrating, and dealing with musical and behavioral situations as they arise.

Studies in early childhood musical development underscore how important it is for teachers to understand certain pedagogical issues related to singing. Graham Welch and others point out that, while singing is a common activity in schools in the early years, teachers rarely are able to attend to the individual needs of their students' singing progress.[1] Singing is usually experienced as a class activity, with a song being sung as a communal enterprise. Although each child makes an individual contribution to the song, it is the whole collective choral sound—the amalgam of those constituent voices—that is heard by the teacher, rather than individual voices with their varying stages of, for example, pitch development. A composite feedback is then likely to be given the class, often (and understandably so) without reference to the particular vocal needs of individual children. This contrasts, of course, with the one-on-one tuition that is usually associated with singing and singing development in conservatories and universities, and also with the individual feedback children will likely receive in, say, their classes in mathematics.

Individuals nevertheless throughout the human age span display a wide range of abilities in terms of pitch-matching behaviors. Consequently, the responsibility of the teacher and conductor with young children remains to provide high-quality feedback as regularly as possible, not only on their ensemble vocal sound, but also on their *individual* vocal needs. It is so much better if this is done as early on in vocal development years as possible, in order to avoid more complex vocal, musical, and even psychological problems later.

Research has shown that in teaching songs to young children, words and music need to be separated in order to avoid difficulties in developing accurate pitch perception. It appears that Western children develop more accurate pitch perception when focusing on it alone, rather than being expected to learn words and music together initially. Teachers and conductors in these contexts might focus on approaching the learning of songs in the style of a "game."[2] While it is to be expected that children will exhibit a range of singing competencies and behaviors at an early stage, conductors and teachers should recognize that this is not necessarily an accurate indication of later singing skills and musical development. Children, adolescents, and adults are all able to improve their singing abilities, including handling pitching. We all can improve, given a normal anatomy and physiology; we just need optimal experiences to help us on our way.

What is the role of the conductor in this respect? Well, many of the philosophical principles permeating this book still apply. First and essentially, we need to remember that everyone is musical or, as Welch puts it, to correct the misunderstanding that human beings are either musical or unmusical. We are by nature musical (see chapters 2 and 3). Conductors and teachers must understand that "out-of-tune singing" occurs when there is a mismatch between the musical task and the individual's current singing competence. Poor teaching and an inappropriate view of musical ability can confirm a state of "out-of-tune singing" in a child or adult. We all know people who have failed to move along the continuum of singing competence because of some thoughtless word from a teacher or parent, an erroneous view of musical ability, or just plain bad teaching. Too many of the people who have such poor perceptions of their singing abilities believe that this state is irreversible.

Many people, including some teachers, think that poor singing ability is an indication of poor general level of musical competence. Susan Knight in her study on adult "non-singers" suggests that this belief is an embedded cultural myth. In her research she found common threads in the narratives of non-singing adults, the labeling of themselves as non-singers being self-attributed. Specifically these threads were:

1. Non-singing adults seem to believe they do not and have never had the ability to sing.
2. The belief that they are non-singers most often arose in their childhood, often through a negative defining ensemble experience, and often involving an authority figure as the instrument of diagnosis.
3. In social situations, they are often self-declarative about their non-singing state, and their narrative often takes the form of self-deprecating humor.
4. The marginalization/exclusion arising from their non-singing status often leads to regret and may have had a deleterious effect on other aspects of their adult lives.
5. Although non-singing adults may wish that they could sing, they seem to believe that their non-singing state is irrevocable, irreversible.[3]

Following community extension courses for some of these non-singing students at her university in Canada, Knight reports heartrending stories of people who were led to believe that they have no singing ability being amazed by their newfound skills: "In singing class, I can be overcome by emotion so easily. Just facing the years of hurt and the amazing belief that I can sing after all. (Elizabeth, age 62)."

Many people have sadly spent most of their lives believing that they cannot sing. By providing the appropriate educational setting, however, we can enhance the singing skills of children and adults. Singing classes, specifically for those who perceive themselves as non-singers, could be an important way of engaging unconfident people in the activity within a safe educational environment. People young and old simply need the opportunity.

The importance and value of high-quality feedback was outlined in chapter 2. Here are some of the ways in which conductors and teachers with young children can give such feedback and therefore ensure individual as well as collective vocal and musical development[4]:

- Encourage and check for *good posture,* which embraces:

  —a lengthened back (tall and straight but not rigid)
  —shoulders relaxed, arms relaxed (not poker straight and rigid)
  —breastbone up
  —eyes looking forward
  —jaws relaxed
  —breathing from the abdominal area (shoulders and collarbone should not move or be raised when taking in breath).

- Think of *making sense of the words* by trying not to breathe in the middle of phrases.
- Encourage the use of appropriate and effective *dynamics* in the singing to help present the meaning of the songs and avoid shouting in loud passages.
- Avoid songs with a large vocal range to begin with, in order to foster accurate pitching.
- Start each class with something the singers know and feel comfortable with to ensure a positive approach to learning new songs; also finish on a "high" with something they have learned well.
- Use a wide range of *imagery and analogy* to help produce appropriate vocal timbre and musical expression. (These will be far more effective and expedient than a barrage of technical terms that may be misconstrued.)
- Make the conducting *gesture* simple and appropriate to the character of the music. Play games with conducting to help the

singers focus (e.g., with tempi and cut-offs); let them hear the difference.

- Be positive and encouraging and adjust inaccuracies in the context of taking target practice and not admonishment.
- Separate the words and music in the learning process (using any sounds—"ma," "loo," for example—will also enable the conductor to focus on and explore different vocal *timbres*).
- Provide a vocal model through *demonstration* with the young singers matching pitches, including pitch glides (glissandi) to gain mastery in pitch development. (Research experiments have revealed that (a) a child's vocal pitch model is a more accurate model than an adult's; (b) female vocal pitch models are better than male; (c) non-vibrato models are more effective with out-of-tune singers than are models with vibrato.)[5]
- Give as much individual *feedback* as possible during the early years within a safe environment to promote and ensure positive vocal development.

The concentration on the *musical* features of a song will enable young singers to feel safe, as opposed to dealing with the technical issues and thus pointing out mistakes. The breathing of a phrase and the expressive qualities of a song should be the concern of all conductors and teachers. Young children will be able to connect with the story or expression of a song more easily than with its technical aspects. That is not to say we don't attend to these, as we certainly don't want inaccuracies to become embedded, but rather we can move toward technical accuracy through the musical demands of each song.

ADOLESCENT SINGING DEVELOPMENT

While many of the principles outlined in relation to singing development in the early years are relevant to all ages, there are specific issues that pertain in particular to adolescence. The obvious and most noticeable feature of vocal development at this age is, of course, voice change. It occurs in both males and females, but more prominently in males. Voice change coincides with the onset of puberty, where major changes in anatomy occur. The age of puberty varies, with the males normally changing between the ages of 9.5 and 14 years and females between the ages of 8 and 15 years. Voice change is most active between 12.5 years and 14 years.[6] This provides challenges for choral conductors and teachers particularly in the school environment. The changing voice maturation process occurs at a time when many other adolescent cultural, social, sexual, and physiological issues are on display.

Many years ago, when I was Director of Music at a London secondary school (teaching students between the ages of 11 and 18), I recall having debates (not quite arguments) with a parent of two very musical boys in the school. The parent requested that his younger son stop singing during the period when his voice was changing and wouldn't allow him to continue in the school choir. I objected, not just for selfish reasons of losing a singer (and a talented one at that), but because I had an instinctive belief that boys should continue to sing during the voice transformation, with the proviso that we explore very carefully their ranges and which voice parts they should accordingly sing. Unfortunately for me it was instinct, and at that point in my professional life I could not refer to the more scientific research studies that would have supported my view. The father, by the way, was a voice professor at the Royal Academy of Music in London! So, I didn't really have a leg to stand on, but we nevertheless remained on good terms, and the father sang solo roles for us from time to time. The younger son eventually went on to Cambridge University and sang in the King's College Chapel Choir.

However, there is now some useful research that gives us insight into the nature of the adolescent voice and how to deal with it in pedagogical and musical terms. John Cooksey has carried out extensive longitudinal studies across the United States and in other parts of the world into the voice transformation of adolescent males.[7] He presents some general points about male voice change that teachers need to be aware of, namely that:

- Voice change occurs at the onset of puberty and is related to the development of primary and secondary sexual characteristics.
- Irregular growth rates in the vocal mechanism can make the voice unpredictable and difficult to control, particularly if it is forced into the wrong pitch range.
- Between the ages of 12 and 15, boys' voices are in varying stages of growth and development.
- The rate of vocal change varies among individuals.

Conductors and teachers not only need to understand the nature of voice change themselves, but they should help young male singers to understand their own voices during the change by

- explaining what is happening vocally and physiologically.
- listening to individual voices in order to classify them in appropriate vocal ranges.
- establishing and maintaining good singing habits.

Following his research, Cooksey has identified six distinct stages of vocal maturation in the adolescent male. He presents a suitable pitch range and tessitura, indicating the most comfortable pitches in that range, in each stage of change.

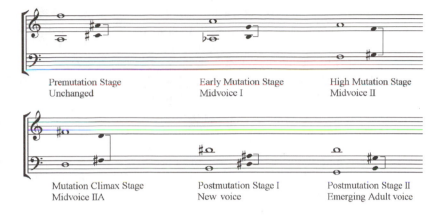

| Premutation Stage | Early Mutation Stage | High Mutation Stage |
| Unchanged | Midvoice I | Midvoice II |

| Mutation Climax Stage | Postmutation Stage I | Postmutation Stage II |
| Midvoice IIA | New voice | Emerging Adult voice |

The rate at which boys move through the maturation stages varies from individual to individual and can take varying times at each stage. Nonetheless, the process is predictable and logical. The stages can be defined in terms of range, tessitura, register development, voice quality, and speaking voice fundamental frequency. Changing voices, as Cooksey points out, become less agile and are more vulnerable to vocal abuse.

The implications for teachers and conductors of choirs that include adolescent boys are profound. It is challenging to deal with a choir that includes the full range of the vocal stages of development at one time! Not only will a lot of choral repertoire be inappropriate for accommodating the vocal ranges, but even certain unison songs may present difficulties for certain boys. While boys are finding their voices and new ranges, it is important to bear in mind some of the vocal development issues that will present excessive challenge. Bach's *Mass in B minor* (and indeed a lot of Bach's choral music) is not the most appropriate music for developing adolescent singers, because the music is usually full of long phrases and melodies with extensive pitch leaps. (OK, that is another extreme example—but it makes the point.) More suitable music might have shorter phrases and more stepwise melodic lines in order for the singers to feel comfortable in their new vocal ranges. Examples of more suitable music might include Dawson's arrangement of the spiritual *Ev'ry Time I Feel the Spirit*, Handel's chorus *How Excellent Thy Name* from *Saul*, and Pitoni's motet *Cantate Domino*.

Emily Crocker's three-part arrangement of Purcell's *Come, Ye Sons of Art*, for example, sits within unchanged (high), midvoice II (middle), and new voice (low) ranges outlined by Cooksey. This kind of arrangement of some of the classic choral repertoire, which accommodates three rather than four (the conventional soprano, alto, tenor, and bass) parts, may well be more suitable for the middle school or junior high school age range. Arrangements such as these also bring the young singers in touch with quality music. It is not impossible to find music, but it will take time if we want to accommodate the developing voices of our young male singers within a comfort zone.

Young men need to feel able to sing and also to feel comfortable about it. They can easily become embarrassed and put off if they find singing awkward or uncomfortable; and we do not want vocal *effort* to be rehearsed, lest it become a lifelong habit. As with swimming or other physical activities, a whole series of bad habits can be nurtured and developed that make the activity hard work and inefficient. Adolescence is a delicate time and it is incumbent on teachers and conductors to nurture students during the maturational stages.

It is important for the conductor to spend time with young males to develop good vocal tone production. They will need much encouragement and positive reinforcement of their developing good habits. In addition, I have noticed that young males respond to encouragement and like to know how their own voice is developing. Having also watched John Cooksey testing and "classifying" boys' voices, it is exciting to see how interested they become in their own vocal maturation.

On one occasion, while observing a trainee teacher in a challenging inner city London school teaching the Zulu part song *Sya Hamba* to a class of 12-year-olds, I sat next to a boy who clearly was more physically mature than average for the age group. He was a very inexperienced singer and was finding difficulty in matching pitch, his voice certainly being in advanced stages of change. After some time repeatedly singing the baritone part next to him and giving him various visual as well as aural cues, he gradually joined in with me with slow but increasing success in pitch accuracy. When I told him that I thought he was a bass singer, he bristled with pride—"I'm a bass, I'm a bass," he exclaimed—and left the class clearly with a degree of self-esteem that he did not have before in his singing and musical development. Boys respond favorably to singing in parts—two or three parts—so teachers should encourage different groupings and avoid just singing in unison.

In addition to the pointers provided for the early years, other suggestions for dealing with adolescent singers include:

- Begin vocal exercises and vocalizes in the most comfortable singing area of the range (this might differ from stage to stage).

- Educate young male singers about the physiology of their voice, the process of maturation, and their own vocal capabilities.
- Be aware of and look out for signs of vocal stress; avoid long periods of rehearsal and singing.
- Regard and deal with voice change in a positive manner as a healthy and natural phenomenon.

Voice change in the adolescent female is not as dramatic as the males' change, but it does occur. It might best be described as "shades of change." Lynne Gackle has made an equivalent study to Cooksey's with female vocal maturation,[8] and, while there is less perceptible change in vocal ranges as compared with males, differences are highlighted in terms of timbre and quality. She points out that adolescent female voice change can be characterized by

- a lowering of the average speaking pitch area
- some voice cracking and abrupt register breaks
- increased breathiness, huskiness, or hoarseness in vocal quality
- decreased and inconsistent range capabilities (tessitura tends to fluctuate)
- uncomfortable singing or rather too much effort and delayed onset of phonation
- heavy, breathy, and rough tone production and/or a colorless, breathy, and thin tone quality
- insecurity in pitch intonation

Gackle supports the idea of making sure that musical literature is appropriate for adolescents and not too childlike or unchallenging. Conductors and teachers need to pay attention to the text of songs to ensure appropriateness. Also, setting suitable challenges is important in order to maintain the interest of young female singers, as is teaching particular concepts such as phrasing, diction, and musical interpretation and expressive singing that stem from the chosen repertoire. For these reasons, teachers and conductors should use unison singing with girls to focus musical line, phrasing, and dynamics. They should also change the seating to allow adolescent girls to hear different vocal models around them, and use music in which parts are similar in range and therefore interchangeable. By gaining an understanding of the musical and expressive requirements of the repertoire, the concept of vocal tone and choral blend will gradually take on new dimensions for the young singers.

While it is clear that much care and attention is needed when dealing with adolescent male and female singers, one strong message is that they do not need to be patronized or left unchallenged musically. Give them quality music in whatever style or genre. This was also a message that was given to me by one high school choral director in Utah. I was invited to be a clinician at a festival, and was amazed to see this one high school with a choir of 200: 100 males and 100 females! I asked the director what made them attend his choir, as he appeared in the warm-up rehearsal to have a rather dictatorial and aggressive manner (confounding all my theories about making singers feel comfortable). He said that he gave them only quality music. On that occasion they had performed exquisitely and from memory the *Kyrie* from Mozart's *Requiem* and the *Agnus Dei* from Byrd's *Mass for Five Voices*—quality music and challenging repertoire by any standards.[9]

In conclusion, conductors should ensure the music they select lies comfortably within suitable vocal ranges; where necessary they should be prepared to make adjustments and arrangements in order to promote successful and effective performance. Allow the music to serve our human needs at this stage of development. The important thing we as conductors can give our young singers is the wherewithal to feel good about their voices and for them to want to continue singing into and throughout adulthood. Increased understanding of the adolescent voice will enable this to happen.

THE AGING VOICE

Many community and church choirs have singers in their middle age and older. People are living longer and have more leisure and retirement time. Singing has become a popular and important activity for them. We sometimes conjure up in our minds a stereotype of the older voice—perhaps one lacking in focus or definition with a wide and slow vibrato, or one that is louder than it ideally should be. While there are acoustic changes associated with the aging voice, there is no reason that the voices in older adults should not remain in a healthy and expressive state for many years. It is more likely that a voice will remain in a good condition if the general health of the older adult is good. There is enough research evidence to show that there is no reason for well-conditioned and healthy voices not to have similar characteristics to much younger voices.[10] It would seem that vocal training and experience can counteract any deterioration normally associated with the advancing age.

What does this mean for the choral conductor with choirs of aging voices? It would seem that the most important thing is to convince the singers that it is possible to continue singing. I remember when I first started with my community choir, a sprightly 83-year-old contralto came up to me after one rehearsal and asked me quite bluntly to tell her when I thought she ought to go. In fact, this particular singer had sung frequently all her life, including, she told me, with Sir Henry Wood (a famous British conductor and founder of the London Promenade Concerts). Her voice was as agile and focused as the voices of singers 30 years her junior; her sight-reading skills were acute, and she hardly ever took her eye off me. She was the last alto I wanted to leave!

However, more delicate situations do arise. Conductors sometimes have to deal with singers whose individual contribution is not always in the interests of the whole choir. There is no easy answer here. Regular "voice placements" in choirs (I use this phrase instead of "audition," because it has less harsh connotations for singers) might help to *re*place singers. I felt recently that one tenor, who was also 83 years old, was unable to control his dynamic range very effectively and therefore was more noticeable vocally within the overall balance and blend of the choir. During the voice placement, I asked him to move to the bass section, commenting positively on his wide vocal range. Here his voice blended more successfully with the others in the section and became less obvious. Nobody lost face in what could have been a very delicate situation. He had told me on many occasions how much the choir meant to him; how could I ask him to leave?

In a large choir, it is often possible to hide particular voices. I also spend time "placing" singers within each voice part. I use some rehearsal time to do this and while, for example, placing the sopranos in relation to each other, I ask the rest of the choir if they notice a difference in the vocal blend when certain voices stand in front of or behind others. This is an interesting acoustical exercise and one that can make a difference to the overall sound (see the section on Spacing and Acoustics in chapter 7). Involving the rest of the choir in decision making has the advantage of shared ownership of the enterprise, and gives singers and the conductor an opportunity to hear the sounds in relation to each other. This is preferably done in groups of four or five singers, and then voices can be judiciously placed to the best advantage of the whole choral sound.

Many of the strategies used with young singers outlined earlier in this chapter are still appropriate for the older singers. Good, healthy posture, deep abdominal breathing, and expressive singing all contribute to the maintenance of healthy singing. General well being with aerobic exercises balanced with appropriate rest, good diet, and an active and young mind—the whole bodymind approach to life—can ensure expressive singing potential for older adults. What matters also is the social interaction and sense of identity gained from being in a communal gathering of singers. In terms of rehearsing, it will be important for the conductor to warm up the voices in careful stages, as with younger or any voices for that matter, and reinforce all the good habits of singing.

IMPORTANT INFLUENCES ON SINGING

Throughout the book I have stressed that conductors and teachers have significant influence on singers and their singing abilities, musical and vocal outcomes, and on the self-perception of those they conduct and teach. This is noticeably so in the early years of singing, when adults' beliefs and perceptions about their singing abilities are often established, as Susan Knight poignantly illustrates in her research. There are, nevertheless, several factors that can directly impede or enhance progress in singing development that have been alluded to in both philosophical and practical terms over the course of the book. Our pedagogical approach can indeed be of utmost importance in this respect.

Graham Welch in *Onchi and Singing Development* provides a number of factors that define and influence the nature of singing:

1. *sociocultural factors,* including social class; gender; location of home, school, and community; ethnicity; opportunities for singing within the culture; and links with language and language development
2. *physical and maturational factors,* which include the basic physical structure, its size and effect on vocal sound, the hearing mechanism, inappropriate physical behavior patterns, stress, physical changes, significant growth periods, and aging
3. *psychological factors,* including cognitive issues, self-perception, self-labeling and stress-related problems
4. *musical factors* related primarily to the complexity of the music and its suitability for the age range
5. *pedagogical factors*[11]

While conductors and teachers need to be aware of all the potential influences on the nature of singing, pedagogical factors deserve special attention. Among them:

1. It is unlikely that much time will be given to conducting and singing even for specialist music teachers in secondary education. This may not necessarily be the case; I was given the opportunity while working at the University of Maryland, for example, to teach a choral methods class even to instrumental majors in music education. This addressed issues of conducting, rehearsing, vocal development, and choral arranging. But it is in initial teacher education that much important groundwork can be covered, including establishing appropriate attitudes toward the whole area of choral education. For non-specialist teachers who are still likely to be involved with singing activity with younger children, there is little time within teacher education courses to begin to address some

of these issues. Professional development therefore is integral to moving toward a greater understanding of choral education; so much so that my colleagues and I have designed a choral education graduate program (see chapter 10).

2. The nature and complexity of the singing and vocal task is something that Welch addresses with particular reference to accuracy of pitch matching. It is suggested that *pitch movement* comes before *pitch matching*. Basically, young singers should be given opportunities to explore vocally, using pitch contours with slides and glides and then moving on to increasing accuracy with pitch matches. Further strategies to improve pitch matching include *echoing* and *antiphoning* methods of teaching songs.[12]

3. The vocal model provided by teachers and conductors should offer appropriate vocal timbres or pitches to match. We know that non-vibrato voices, for example, give a more accessible and accurate model than voices with an extensive vibrato. Female vocal models are better than male models, especially with young children with unchanged voices. This might beg the question as to whether male conductors and teachers should model using their *falsetto* range when dealing with pitching matters.

4. We need to ensure that developing singers are provided with high-quality feedback on vocal and musical matters.

Educators hardly need reminding of the potential we have to enhance or damage young people's development in any curriculum or subject area. Conductors need to know that their influence on people's lives is equally potent. In my first teaching job, I recall one young boy who was very enthusiastic about everything and wanted to sing in every choir and play as many instruments as possible. His pitch accuracy was not everything a conductor could wish for at the age of 12, but as he progressed, and with appropriate encouragement, he improved remarkably over his school years. It would have been so easy to dampen his enthusiasm by negative comments. Now he is a professional opera singer, singing major roles in the opera houses of Europe and North America, including Covent Garden and the Met.

Singing for *all* people is a *continuum* of development. We can all travel along that continuum. Teachers and conductors have an awesome responsibility to ensure that individual and collective singing development occurs and that music is not performed at the expense of those human needs.

10

TEACHING CHORAL CONDUCTING: PHILOSOPHY AND PRACTICE

WHAT CAN WE TEACH?

Can we teach conducting? While some conductors themselves believe it is a God-given gift, that there is a mystique about conducting, we would not expect even the most talented instrumentalist or vocalist to go without teaching or coaching. There is always more to learn, but learning is not the result only of teaching. Learning is something that we do all the time; we learn through experience as well as occasionally through instruction. I believe that conductors need some other musical experience before they begin to conduct. But I don't hold with the view that just because you are an organist you are de facto a potentially effective choral conductor or choral trainer. There is an underlying assumption that conducting is something that you just do—to keep the singers singing together. Easy!

Clearly for some, conducting comes more naturally and easily than for others. Nowhere is this more apparent than in the many conducting classes I have taught in universities. Some student conductors have a natural sense of movement of the body in their gestures and posture, whereas others feel, and therefore look, more awkward and less comfortable. Naturally able or talented conductors need to be nurtured, in the same way that we would nurture instrumentalists and vocalists. Indeed, through teaching conducting both at undergraduate and graduate levels, I have come to learn a lot about conducting, music, singing, and human beings, including myself.

In order to motivate and get the best out of student conductors, we have to make them feel good about themselves mentally, emotionally, and kinesthetically. They have to be free from any baggage that gets in the way of allowing them to be expressive with gesture. This often involves thinking of the connections between the body's natural movement and the technical particulars of conducting gestures. Many conducting students are stuck in a physical modus operandi. This is especially true of more experienced conductors, or at least those who have got into particular and often inappropriate habits of posture, stance, or gestures. Like the swimming habits I described at the beginning of the book, it is more difficult to disentangle ourselves from bad habits the longer we have been engaged in them. Whether it is swimming, leaving the cap off the toothpaste, or using a particular conducting posture, our behaviors require very conscious efforts to change once we have formed habits in our bodyminds. This is true of singers *and* conductors, some of whom seem unable to operate unless their arms are lifted high, tension appears in the neck, or a host of other weird and seemingly uncomfortable postures are taken.

One singing teacher told me of a student who simply could not sing unless he was standing with his head to one side. He had for years been a chorister in an Oxford college chapel, where the singers had to look to the side instead of straight ahead in order to be able to see the conductor, because the choir stalls faced inward along the side of the chapel. His bodymind had programmed this stance securely, and it would take some conscious reprogramming to enable him to adopt what we would all consider a more normal and comfortable posture for singing. A conducting student of mine for many years had conducted with her arms lifted rather high, causing tension along the side of her body, neck, and shoulders. Even after repeated work on posture during one session, each time she started to conduct she resumed her accustomed stance. Careful and conscious adjustment over a long period of time were necessary for her to find the newer posture comfortable and normal. Her review of video recordings of her conducting were helpful in making the adjustment. These examples also illustrate the diplomacy and delicacy that teaching requires when dealing with very personal issues and habits.

In the design of choral conducting courses, an underlying rationale must be presumed, so that they become more than just technical, beat-pattern style courses. The essential technical and musical requisites need to be addressed, of course, but alongside communication skills and the expressive and stylistic musical requirements. After all, we are dealing with musical, technical, personal, and communication issues that are all integral to successful conducting. Teachers ideally need the opportunity to reflect on their teaching and courses, and to this end written rationales and descriptions help to codify thinking and beliefs. This will help students and teachers to consider in practice their own paradigms. However, it is not always easy to determine whether any success is due to the teaching technique or the inherent personality and skills of the conductor. This question is the concern of teachers of any subject in relation to the success of their students; how much of the success of students is due to the teaching and how much is elicited by the students' own motivation, skills, and personalities. But teaching *can* make a difference and, at the very least, promote personal reflection on the activity.

In designing choral conducting courses, we need to bear in mind there will be differing conducting and rehearsing needs depending on the conducting and singing contexts. But we also can develop a list of the constituent elements that make up the effective conducting course, just as we did for the conductor (see chapter 6). Inextricable linkage must be made between the act of conducting and the integral skills of rehearsing. I prefer this linkage to be made clear and maintained throughout conducting courses.

From his research on the development and application of a model for the teaching of conducting gestures, Dale Lonis outlined a table of activities and skills that ought to be considered for inclusion in a conducting program.[1] He categorizes the identified skills under *cognitive, affective,* and *psychomotor* processes, according to Benjamin Bloom's taxonomy of educational objectives and learning theories.[2] He relates these to Bloom's belief that, in order to make a skill automatic through practice, educators planning training courses must clearly define those basic skills that are required to bring about the desired outcomes.

However, the assumption may be made that failure to apply some or all of these skills would render the conductor to a degree ineffective; that can be the problem with any list. While I have some difficulty with itemizing specific technical elements of conducting and certainly do not believe they can be taught without a contextual reference to particular music, it might be helpful, nevertheless, to list some of them at this stage. But we should understand and recall from chapter 2 that we cannot and do not separate cognitive, affective, and psychomotor processes in our musical operations. We do not process our musical experiences (or others) in that simplistic way. Please think holistically. Some of the *cognitive* processes that might be listed are concerned with basic theory skills and aural skills, including

- note and chord recognition, harmonic structure and language
- time signature, note length, pulse recognition
- key signature, tonal center, intonation recognition

- instrumentation and transposition recognition, voice range, and tessituras
- musical language usage, technical term recognition

The *affective* processes tend to be concerned with the comprehension of feelings in order to make music appropriately expressive from musical notation, and might include

- melodic, rhythmic, harmonic, and timbre affect of particular performance practices
- absolute or referential basis of historical/theoretical perspective for aesthetic understanding
- aesthetic awareness of performance practice as it affects each performance

The *psychomotor* processes tend to be concerned with basic physical gestures required to communicate intent or interpretation of the music, and might include:

- stance
- preparatory gestures
- releases
- left and right hand control and independence
- beat patterns
- cues
- expressive gestures

While many of the skills outlined here will be intuitive for a number of student conductors, the identification of appropriate skills and processes will promote further insight into the nature of effective conducting and the recognition of ineffectiveness. This is a useful list, but they are not sequential skills and processes that can be checked off when achieved. Nor are they skills that are isolated from one another. We certainly need to understand, for example, meter, time signatures, and pulse recognition as conductors, which are generally skills considered under the cognitive umbrella. But we surely cannot separate them from the doing—the conducting of the meter and time signatures—which are essentially psychomotor processes and which conductors must *feel*. Also, to understand and feel the meter and pulse of, for example, a sarabande, the *affective* domain and aesthetic awareness are involved. All the processes are inextricably connected.

There is, for my liking, too much emphasis on checklist-style "learning objectives" throughout the educational system. It is not just a question of whether the students have managed to gain mastery of all the skills and processes outlined, but rather whether they are able to *apply* such skills when appropriate and, key to it all, *recognize* the need for such application. Can we reliably establish that learning has taken place without some sort of contextual reference—in our case the rehearsal? We may have student conductors with the keenest aural abilities, but unless those students can use those abilities within a human-compatible context, they will not be put to optimum use. Other student conductors may have all the communication skills in the world, but without a musical ear that can identify what is happening in the music, they will be largely ineffective in rehearsal. A student may have gained control and independence of the right and left hands when conducting, but that student will need to know what that independence means and when it can be employed naturally and effectively. Another student may have a wonderfully appropriate posture and stance, but it is inconsequential without clear preparation gestures and musical know-how. A teaching curriculum for conducting will include all the theoretical and aural skills outlined, insight into musical expression, as well as the postural and gestural motor skills. But there must be linkage among them all. To teach a student how to conduct three in a bar is perfunctory unless we know the *kind* of three in a bar the music requires; that is understanding and feeling the music.

To expand on this a little further and referring back to the supermodel, an effective conductor must first have a collection of technical skills pertaining to the ability to recognize musical features aurally (such as inaccuracies in rhythm or pitch, inappropriate balance). Choral conductors will be ineffective if they are unable, for example, to recognize inaccurate notes and chords sung in a rehearsal, because these will need to be adjusted. The education of conductors should, consequently, include aural skill training.

Knowledge and understanding of the context of the music historically and theoretically and its appropriate aesthetic potential is another prerequisite of an effective conductor. If conductors do not have such knowledge and understanding underpinning their work, then it is likely that the performance will not reach its optimum level. The basic psychomotor skills and processes already outlined are related to the communication of the musical elements through physical gestures, which in the case of the ineffective conductor will be unclear, ambiguous, and confusing to the singer. We don't want to give our singers mixed messages. A taxonomy of conducting activities, skills, and behaviors will certainly be useful in helping students to focus on, practice, and learn the elements that contribute to the whole. However, is it possible to conclude that the outlined skills represent the totality of attributes necessary for a conductor to be effective? Does such a list obviate the notion of mystique (those more unidentifiable elements) of effective conducting?

While teachers can be very knowledgeable about their subjects, or have well-developed technical skills, it does not follow that they will be able to transmit such knowledge effectively to their students. Poor ability to communicate with the students is likely to destimulate motivation and lessen their interest level. So conductors may have sufficient musical skills without the ability to communicate and use such skills effectively. What actually constitutes communication skills in the conducting context? Can we define a paradigm here?

One key communication skill is through demonstration, explanation, and imaginative use of imagery and analogy in rehearsals as means of enhancing the expressive quality of music. Certain research has investigated and analyzed how specific observed behaviors—for example, eye contact, facial expressions, and use of voice—contribute to the overall success of the conductor's communication skills. Less concerned with such atomistic detail, some research identifies the general personality of the conductor as being the real catalyst for successful communication. Strouse, for example, maintained that a positive personality and competent rehearsal skills led to a meaningful musical performance, and that knowledge of the musical score and secure technique will enhance the conductor's confidence.[3] Strouse's thesis supports a conception that aesthetic awareness, musical knowledge, technical skills, and positive personality all contribute to a conductor's overall effectiveness. In the book *Conscience of a Profession*, the choral director and teacher Howard Swan endorses such principles and outlines the varying functions and roles of the choral conductor:

> He is an *organizer* of time and activity, a *technician* as he works with the tonal and musical resources of his choir, a *communicator* of musical ideas to the performer and auditor, a *listener* to all kinds of live and recorded performance, and *educator* as he attempts to make those about him understand and appreciate musical values, a *scholar* and an *interpreter* of that which is found in the score.[4]

This gives us a real clue as to what is entailed in conducting and therefore in teaching conducting. We need to be able to *organize* our rehearsals in terms of timing and pacing of the activities; planning and preparation is integral to this. Swan also suggests we *listen* to other choirs and performances in order to gauge our own choirs, but also to be open-minded to different interpretations of music; this is the *interpreter* and *scholar* role. We need to explore new music and discover ways of reinterpreting well-worn pieces in our repertoire to remind us that music is a living phenomenon. The *educator* role, I hope, is permeating choral philosophy and practice.

Anecdotes about the great conductors do not mention necessarily, or even at all, just the clarity of their beat or other discrete technical elements, but rather focus on a quintessence of their behaviors, principles, and actions. So it is perhaps the whole that should be considered in the teaching curriculum. Observing and noting specific behaviors, for example, in a rehearsal situation or performance, will not give many clues to the overall effectiveness of that individual conductor. Who will determine what are effective and appropriate behaviors? What may be a relevant behavior in one rehearsal may not be in another. A conductor may feel the need to concentrate in one rehearsal on, say, vocal production, while in another more on pitch accuracy. That is not to say that one rehearsal is better or is more effective than another, but rather that conductors respond to the needs of the choir as perceived at different times. In one rehearsal the conductor may intentionally tackle small details, with extensive use of verbal language and repetition, while in another she may intentionally facilitate a run-through of the whole program with little attention to detail, technical accuracy, or vocal production. Both are valid rehearsal activities. Effective musical gesture may not always appear in each rehearsal, yet it is considered an important and natural ingredient of the effective choral conductor as a whole. This suggests that the observation of conductors in only one rehearsal might be somewhat unrepresentative of the total picture. How we teach that presents the challenge. How students learn what to do is the craft of teaching and conducting: teaching is about presenting students with informed choice.

Effectiveness will be framed by the context in which the rehearsal is taking place; what will be appropriate for the conductor of a school choir will likely be different from that of a professional choir or a large symphony chorus. So many factors contribute to the essence of effective conducting that it would seem difficult and even unnecessary to measure small distinct aspects without relating to the totality. Effectiveness as a concept can only be meaningful within the context of the musical aims of the activity in process. In a school choir of young singers, we have to be aware of pacing the rehearsal by not giving them time to become distracted, and by offering variety within each rehearsal by ensuring that, largely through repetition, music gets learned. On reflection, it's not so different with adults!

CONSTRUCTING A CURRICULUM

The construction of a choral conducting curriculum will be dependent naturally on the level of the students. Those who are starting from scratch—perhaps undergraduate students who do not have much opportunity for consistent practice—will have different needs from, say, graduate students who are already practicing with choirs on a regular basis. I will outline a conducting curriculum for both; one for more or less ab initio students and the other for the professional development of the more advanced. The first will be largely concerned with developing the basic skills and knowledge of conducting, while the other will encourage reflection on practice. At both levels critical self and peer analysis should be encouraged through the use of video recording and as much "lab" work as possible.

Developing interpersonal and communication skills in conducting students, or at least heightening awareness of the need for them, is difficult. Let's assume and hope that conducting teachers themselves have keen communication skills for starters. Building an awareness of what behavioral traits and actions are appropriate for choral singing is, I believe, necessary for students. In the same way that hospital doctors should be expected to develop a suitable bedside manner for their patients, so choral conductors need to gain mechanisms and strategies to establish an environment in which their singers do not feel threatened.

David Elliott puts forward six strategies highlighting a model of student-teacher interactions. These strategies are constructive ways of considering teaching methodology in the context of developing choral communication skills in student conductors in particular, though also in music education practice in general:

- *Modeling:* a process of reciprocal teaching and learning in which the students can observe good practice and the teacher moves the students toward the model
- *Coaching:* interaction between student and teacher as the task is being performed, involving talking, reminding, prompting, and moving students toward the artistic goal
- *Scaffolding:* support of students in their endeavors and consequent *fading* of the teacher's role
- *Articulating:* expression by students of their musical ideas and solutions to problems
- *Comparative reflection:* encouragement of the student to consider other ideas as an alternative to fulfilling the musical aim
- *Exploring:* identification of "sub-goals" and "sub-problems," enabling students to take ownership of the musical activity[5]

Elliott's six strategies of model student-teacher interactions provide a strong basis for teaching conducting. First, students need to engage in the activity by being conducted by good conductors themselves; this also forms part of the analysis of practice. Then coaching is clearly part of any practical activity—swimming or conducting—by moving toward the goals set by the teacher. The teacher supports the students throughout the enterprise by eventually becoming less prominent in the interaction between the two. Throughout, reflection on practice is key, as is providing a framework and articulating discoveries and ideas. This process also involves exploration of gestures and strategies, and both teachers and students need to feel comfortable about mutual exploration. What may work for one conductor, may not work so well for another: we are all different.

Student conductors will need practice at interacting with their singers in order to know what is effective. The ideal interaction includes the creation of a positive learning environment through an acceptance of the singers' abilities, coupled with setting realistic musical challenges. Student conductors will have to understand that interactions with singers will be more effective when there is a setting that

- provides for and encourages honesty and respect for all people they conduct
- accepts everyone as unique, growing, and developing singers regardless of their behavior
- balances the needs of the individual singers and the needs of the choir

However, these settings are also desirable ones for conducting teachers and their students; the model provided for student conductors by their teachers cascades into the students' practice with their singers. In many of the successful choral interactions between conductors and singers that I have observed over the years, these conditions that maintain human-compatible learning are in place. It would seem to me that it is not just the personality of the conductor that promotes dynamic interaction in the choral rehearsal, but more particularly the interpersonal skills, although we do know from particular research findings that extroverted teachers somehow enable student progress in music more effectively than introverted ones.[6] Therefore, students should be encouraged to act in a more extroverted manner when rehearsing their singers. Video recording of rehearsals can be an effective way of managing the analysis, discussions, and reflections of actions and behaviors to see if conductors actually present the desired image.

Basic communication skills such as facial expressions, eye contact, and use of humor deserve attention because these are the key attributes of dynamic interaction. In conducting classes, the singers always comment when their fellow student conductors do not look at them while conducting, and it is one of the first things they are keen to point out. How can you expect singers to look at the conductor if the conductor fails to look at the singers? This does not always need to be mentioned by the teacher, because the singers will point this out if invited to do so. I believe this is key to effective conducting. It *can* be taught, or at least awareness of the situation, especially through video recording, can be heightened. For some students these will be attributes already in place as part of their own personality; for others it be will be necessary to draw attention to the disadvantages of poor communication skills and work toward improvement (by setting short term sub-goals, for example) as would be done in other, more cognitive areas of learning. Learning in this area *can* occur first through developing awareness of the problem and then seeking ways to adjust behaviors appropriately.

Student conductors often look extensively at the musical score during rehearsals, at the expense of making contact with their singers. Singers do not like this. The clear message is then that conductors must *prepare* the score, know the music, and trust themselves in their knowledge in order to communicate with the singers. There are various ways of preparing the music for rehearsals. One way, naturally, is to get to know all the individual voice parts in order to be able to demonstrate as appropriate any vocal passage. Demonstration is not just about illustrating accurate pitches, but also about vocal timbres and qualities, illustrating perhaps how *not* to do something as well as how to.

There is also knowing the score in its expressive sense; what are the musical phrases doing, how do they connect with the singers' breathing? What are the stylistic considerations? Are we singing Mozart in the style of Rodgers and Hammerstein? Or are we singing Rodgers and Hammerstein in the style of Mozart? Either could be deemed inappropriate. So the student conductor will need to know about musical style and musical conventions. I also believe, as has been threaded through the book, that the conductors should know about the voice and vocal matters in order to be effective and helpful to their singers (again, see the model of an effective choral conductor outlined at the end of chapter 6).

Let's now examine two sample basic course outlines for (1) the undergraduate (or equivalent) novice-level conductor who has limited or no previous experience in conducting and (2) the graduate (or equivalent) more advanced level for the professional development of those already engaged in the practice of conducting. These are ideals framed by my experience teaching courses over some years and adapted from observations of other courses. Variations obviously need to be taken into account to meet particular needs.

Initial Conducting Course

1. The use of natural and expressive body movement to music; principles of non-verbal communication and body language. Development of beat patterns. Resources: variety of music to enable students to develop "natural" movement patterns and conducting shapes.

2. Continuation of exploration of expressive body movement; link with expressive vocal phrasing, text and beat patterns; analysis of structure and character of music. Resources: "simple" vocal music (e.g., Britten's *New Year Carol*) for singing and movement.

3. Demonstration of the integral linkage of conducting with rehearsing. The significance of physical and vocal warm-ups; developing exercises and vocalizes for rehearsal; healthy voice use in relation to gesture and language; gesture and vocal "release." Resources: Vocal warm-ups (e.g., Ehmann & Haasemann; Haasemann & Jordan[7]).

4. Determination of pulse, tempo of music in relation to its natural momentum; starting and ending techniques; changing tempo; aspects of breathing and breath control in relation to gesture. Resources: selection of music with contrasting tempi and expressive style.

5. Conducting patterns; development of gestures with expressive natural framework and traditional patterns; appropriateness of gesture to music. Resources: selection of music with contrasting tempi and expressive style.

6. Conducting styles; gestures as appropriate for styles of music; conducting syncopation, pauses (fermata), conducting complex rhythmic patterns. Resources: music with syncopation (e.g., gospel) and more complex rhythmic patterns (e.g., Rutter's *Shepherd's Pipe Carol*, Bernstein's *America*).

7. Rehearsal strategies: methods of teaching music as appropriate to the choral group; motivation; pacing of rehearsals; conducting in the school contexts. Vocal modeling and demonstration of all voice parts. Resources: unison and part-songs to teach young singers, and other pieces as appropriate (Decker & Kirk;[8] Rao[9]).

8. Rehearsal strategies: continuation of consideration of

strategies; use of imagery, analogy, and demonstration in the choral rehearsal; teaching "challenging" passages—methods and gestures; vocal demonstration while conducting.

9. Conductor as teacher; revision of issues; communication and the choral conductor; repertoire considerations.

Each session will include practical activity and reflection, coupled with discussion of the particular issues. Video recording will be used extensively along with analysis. Although the sessions may appear sequential, the course ideally should take a holistic approach with aspects addressed as appropriate for the needs of the students. The notion that we don't conduct 5/4 time until February is daft. While I clearly would not recommend doing something as complicated as Walton's *Belshazzar's Feast* in an initial conducting course, I have found that students will tackle music that they feel interested in and inspired by and generally rise to the challenge offered by that music. The teacher's role, naturally, is to interfere and influence the proceedings if and when the students have bitten off more than they can chew at this stage in their development.

First of all, I suggest that students are given opportunities to explore and become comfortable with their bodies and gestures. Incorporated into this would be the more formal conducting patterns, for these must become second nature to the students.

It is implicit and necessary that complementary musicianship skills, for example aural training and theory, are developed alongside conducting in other parallel courses.

Advanced Conducting Course

1. Construction of a gesture vocabulary, exploring traditional conducting patterns and other gestures for particular musical and vocal outcomes.
2. Vocal perspectives—the relationship between vocal tone and gesture; how to create particular vocal tones through gesture and other non-verbal means.
3. Rehearsal techniques and strategies; aspects of rehearsal psychology; motivating the singers.
4. The conductor as singer—teacher of singing and vocal model; vocal demonstration.
5. Movement and the choral rehearsal—enhancing musical skills through movement.
6. Gesture and non-verbal communication in the choral rehearsal.

7. Group vocal techniques.
8. Score preparation and musical style; conducting gestures to enhance musical styles; musical challenges.
9. Rehearsal psychology and the interpersonal skills of the conductor.

As with any course on conducting, practical workshop style activities are essential, as are reflection, analysis, and discussion. The use of video recording is very helpful for students to evaluate their own learning and progress. Students would be asked to read and critically review appropriate literature and journal articles for discussion and to connect with practical tasks. These curriculum elements will feature in each session. Again, the sessions should address needs of students as they arise and deal with particular points as required by the chosen music.

It may seem on paper that there is no significant difference between the initial and advanced outlines. However, the major difference concerns the musical challenges set and expectations of outcome. In both courses, a variety of music will be prepared, some pieces presenting rhythmic complexities, some expressive issues with rubato phrasing and other vocal challenges that the conductors will address. Within an educational context, the student conductors will ideally be encouraged to explore gestures, to find out for themselves in their own practice what works successfully and what doesn't, and therefore become confident and trusting in their own conducting and rehearsing.

As part of a whole professional development graduate program, I commend the inclusion of courses on vocal development and singing as well as philosophy and aesthetics. This, from my own experience, has deepened understanding of a whole range of issues connected with conducting. Naturally, further courses on aspects of choral literature itself will be of immense benefit, as will further study on the nature of learning and human behavior.

The course examples are concerned with conducting in the context of rehearsing, not as an abstract phenomenon divorced from singers; perhaps you might consider their having an educational rather than musicological perspective. That is where I come from in writing this book. My philosophy and raison d'etre, if you like, is about connecting music with people.

11

LAST MOVEMENT

Our quest for a model of the effective choral conductor has underscored some of conducting's complexities and issues. Rather like learning to swim, there is much that is natural about the activity, but there is much still to learn. In the same way that swimming can become more efficient, so conducting will benefit from being efficient. The big difference between the two activities is, however, that with conducting we have the potential to influence the musical and emotional lives of other students and choir members, whereas swimming tends to be a lonesome activity, unless, of course you are saving someone from drowning or taking part in some communal water sport. Conducting is not just about waving the arms in the air; gestures are as meaningful as language and have the capacity to create pleasant or ugly sounds. We as conductors can and do influence sound.

It may appear to some as if the book fails to provide hard-and-fast rules about conducting and singing. They would be correct. There is no absolute list of what to do and what not to do; there is no clear sequence offered of what conductors *must* do in a rehearsal, there is no correct way of doing everything. Rather, I approach the text as I do my teaching, by presenting options and giving people choices. We explore, think about the issues, and rationalize, and then we can make informed decisions. This will secure learning more effectively than just blindly following instructions. We all have choices; we can make good ones, or we can make not-so-good ones.

I hope that those who read the book, like the students I teach, will have reflected on their own practice and thought about both the philosophical and practical issues that I have raised. They may well have explored, experimented, and tried things out with their classes and choirs. Please do if you haven't already. I find that choirs are usually eager to try new ideas, new warm-ups, new approaches to singing. I recall some years ago, one very established member of my choir muttering, "Oh God, he's been on another course . . . " when I returned from the summer vacation with some new ideas for physical and vocal warm-ups. Nowadays, I don't hear the mutterings, because the singers *expect* me to have new ideas. They have become receptive to them as, over time, they appreciate the benefits of what may appear at first as idiosyncrasies.

The philosophy of the book is premised on people: getting the best out of them, nurturing, teaching, and making wonderful music with them. We do that largely by creating human-compatible learning situations, not by frightening them with rules and reprimands, but by creating conditions that are safe and free from threat. That is not, of course, to say that our choirs need not be disciplined, well run, and efficient, but that we should aim to provide a tension-free, unstressed environment in which to sing. Indeed, we should be disciplined in the way we run rehearsals: let's start and finish on time, expect keen attention from the singers during the rehearsals, but allow time for socializing and meeting with them as well. Let's be slick in presentation and dressed well, although I do wish we could sometime adopt a "cooler," trendier image; the more formal robes and often very "uncool" dresses used by many choirs might be off-putting for younger potential choir recruits. Let's not create or preserve a stuffy image. I have seen some choirs wearing very imaginatively designed robes and uniforms, in contrast to other choirs wearing very ugly, unflattering ones. It may be that some concerts in particular contexts will be better suited to a more informal dress code, while other contexts clearly call for the more formal attire.

Outreach—another one of today's buzzwords—is, I believe, of fundamental importance. We need to take our wonderful choral music out to the people, rather than sit back and expect them to come to us. This of course is more challenging and needs the support of choir committees as well as the establishment of links with other areas of the community. We hear choirs in hospitals, railway stations, and shopping malls at Christmas, but not so often at other times of the year. We have a wealth of choral repertoire that is other-than-Christmassy, some fine sacred and secular music; we should share it. I am always delighted to hear good instrumental music (and I stress *good*) playing in the streets and underground stations in London, for example, and from time to time solo singers take to performing with karaoke or their own accompaniments; but it is far more seldom we hear choral groups performing out there. The jazz in the streets of New Orleans is legendary. I realize that perhaps I am being extreme again, but the principle seems often to be that choral music should remain in churches or concert halls. (And some of those underground tunnels or metro halls provide excellent resonant environments for singers: but, of course, you should check with your local authorities before possibly breaking the law by performing on the streets!) To increase outreach, choirs could devise programs that include performing in the same concert with other contrasting musical groups; adult choirs could join with children's choirs; choirs could perform in the same concert as a wind or steel band, for example.

Program planning is a major responsibility for conductors and is something that I myself find challenging. I have already referred in previous chapters to the care needed in the planning and preparation of music for adolescent groups in particular. Having looked at the various vocal considerations in planning a program for one concert or for a series of concerts over a year (in chapter 6), we might consider what constitutes good program planning. To maintain that it is just a matter of conductors' tastes is, I believe, to work against the interests of our singers and our audiences. For the average choir to have a diet consisting wholly of sacred music (and clearly I am not referring here to church choirs) will be as limiting as having a season of Handel oratorios or requiems, however exquisite the music might be.

A friend who conducts a highly successful choir in England mentioned recently how difficult he found it to program contemporary music, especially the more esoteric, less tonal works. Even if he "hid" the work among other more accessible music, audiences (especially, he claimed, in more provincial areas) seemed quite reluctant to accept new music. However, he felt it important to perform newly commissioned choral music and made it a general principle that such music should be sung alongside the more popular repertoire.

In a choral concert, other than those with one or two large-scale pieces, it might be useful to reflect on how we program. Is there a theme? Is there an anniversary or other connection with, for example, a particular composer? Is there a focus on the music of one or two particular eras, countries, or composers running through a season? Do we really need to program pieces chronologically? Might it be a good idea to perform pieces that use the same text in one concert? Some years ago, I conducted a concert entitled *Gloria* and performed the settings of the *Gloria* by John Rutter, Vivaldi, and Poulenc. I am currently planning two concerts that will feature the music of Bach alongside twentieth-century American composers—perhaps not so unusual in the United States, but this is

to take place in England! I often like to group pieces together: modern
French with Renaissance English, or spirituals alongside Monteverdi and
Gabrielli. Given below are two sample programs.

SAMPLE 1: Large Community Choir of 120 Singers

Jubilate Deo	Giovanni Gabrielli

Four folk songs sung by a primary school choir of 40 children

Det ar en ros utsprungen	Michael Praetorius/Jan Sandstrom

(an evocative contemporary setting for two choirs of the well-known
Advent chorale)

Five Mystical Songs	Ralph Vaughan Williams
Songs and Cries of London Town	Bob Chilcott

(first performance of specially commissioned work in five short
movements for choir, piano duet, and percussion, which includes
sections for children's choir)

Psalm 100	Heinrich Schütz
Shenandoah	arranged by James Erb
The Battle of Jericho	arranged by Moses Hogan

SAMPLE 2: Chamber Choir of 20 Singers

Program juxtaposing Renaissance and twentieth-century music

O Clap Your Hands	Orlando Gibbons
Four Motets for the Season of Lent	Francis Poulenc
Haec Dies	William Byrd
O Sacrum Convivium	Olivier Messiaen
Bluebird	Charles Villiers Stanford
Le Chant des Oiseaux	Clément Janequin
Ballad of Green Broom	Benjamin Britten
And So It Goes	Billy Joel, arranged by Bob Chilcott

Ideally concerts should not have too many individual pieces of the
same length; it is useful to have a longer work situated in the middle of
a program, particularly if it offers challenges for the singers. Concerts
need to start with something impressive to grab the audience's attention,
and end with something equally impressive or stunning in its beauty
and simplicity for the audience to take away. For example, I have ended
concert programs with the well-known Tallis motet *If Ye Love Me*. In many
ways, choirs are only as good as their last concert or last piece. While a
program with varied musical styles will often present more challenges

for the conductor and choir, the outcome will be very satisfying if the characteristics of each style are captured effectively.

The conductors' responsibilities have been laid out throughout the book for conducting, creating human-compatible learning situations, choosing music, and promoting musical and vocal development in the singers. One of the main elements of this role is, of course, leadership. Singers look to their conductors for leadership musically certainly, but a wider perspective of leadership is expected as well. Conductors are leading their singers potentially to experience something of the sublime; some singers find the singing activity cathartic, liberating, even healing, and it is often a channel for expression of their emotional lives. This is the greatest responsibility, and the conductor can either facilitate or inhibit this experience.

Hilary Apfelstadt suggests that leadership is integral to the creation of an appropriate environment in which quality singing can take place. She proposes three categories of leadership characteristics:

1. "musical": artistic intuition, musicality, and aural sensitivity
2. "extramusical": articulateness, confidence, effort, enthusiasm, initiative
3. "gestalt": combining musical and extramusical elements artfully[1]

The "gestalt" category characterizes a natural leadership role, an elusive quality that make certain people stand out. Rather like political leaders, conductors, by the very nature of the role they undertake, stand out. In his book *Leading Minds,* Howard Gardner studies the leadership characteristics of significant people who throughout the twentieth century have adopted some form of leadership role. He concludes:

> A tension will always exist between those who use their knowledge to manipulate and those who use their knowledge to empower. Political "spinmasters" remind us of this unsettling reality. Yet I believe that the more widely these issues are understood, the less likely it is that irresponsible leadership can rise and prevail in the long run. Moreover, I hope that those who come to appreciate these issues, and who design means of articulating them to a wider audience, will help to usher in a world in which leadership is less coercive, more empowering of the broader citizenry, and better able to achieve constructive ends.[2]

While Gardner is essentially referring to political leadership, there is something that rings true for the leadership styles of conductors.

Conductors, like political leaders or anyone in a sphere of influence, can use their leadership role to manipulate or enable; they can dictate to or empower their singers. They can run their choirs like dictators or adopt a more democratic style of leadership. They can enter the role for their own ends and glorification, or they can facilitate wonderful music making by motivating people. They can in effect become good or poor leaders, teachers, and conductors. The choice is theirs.

I would like to conclude by illustrating how much conductors—and yes, I believe choral conductors in particular—can become a significant part of the lives of their singers. I am sure we can all recount moments when individual performances or even rehearsals have taken on a poignancy that will always be remembered. I would like to thank Regina Carlow for sharing with me one of her particular poignant occasions. As a high school choral director trying to win over her students in a particularly challenging urban environment where she was appointed following the death of her predecessor, Regina found one day that she had to deal with the death of a student in her show choir. Reading her heartrending account makes me realize what an important role we play in the sometimes vulnerable lives of those we conduct.

> One rainy night in February, a speeding car killed Shammara, one of our sopranos, instantly as she was crossing the street. The show choir's grief was overwhelming. Dealing with my own shock was secondary as I began to think what this loss would mean to my students who knew and shared their lives and their choir with this young woman. The Principal announced the tragedy over the school intercom and I was teaching another class at the time. I discovered that many members of the show choir walked out of their classes and one by one came to my room. I later learned that my class was the last time in which many of her friends had seen her alive. I asked the choir how they would like to honor their friend. One of the students suggested that we sing *It's So Hard to Say Goodbye* at her funeral. Our rehearsal for singing at the funeral will always be with me. The students' faces, streaked with tears and swollen from crying, looked out at me as I sat in front of them at the small electric piano during our warm-up. They did not look to me for comfort. They looked to me with a pain that I will always know I was unable to ease. We began the song and suddenly one of the girls let out a cry. I heard the sound of wheels rolling down a wooden floor. The pallbearers were bringing Shammara's casket down the center aisle as we sang. I felt their eyes on me and could feel their lamentation. To mourn is to utter lamentation to

someone. Whereas before, I witnessed their mourning for their former teacher and I bore the brunt of their anger, now I was in their grief with them. I was the *someone* both times, but this time I could view their pain, not be alienated by it. As the pallbearers opened their friend's casket, my choir huddled closer to me yet they continued singing. Once their voice was silent, but now they kept singing. With me, through me, I had become their *muse*.[3]

Whether we operate as Apollo, Pan, or Orpheus, we are in a vital position to help our singers deal with their emotional lives, their loves, their sufferings, their joys, and their angers. We cannot shirk that responsibility. Conductors must be full of empathy, genuineness, and warmth, because without these attributes we are merely mechanical. And that marks the difference between conducting and swimming. In essence, choral conducting is about love.

NOTES

Chapter 1

1. Shaw and D'Angour (1996).
2. Langer (1957).

Chapter 2

1. Much of the material in this chapter is adapted from and documented in Thurman & Welch (2000), 18–26 and 86–301.
2. Cycles of brain growth spurts and their implications for human learning are described and documented in Thurman & Welch (2000), 143–147.
3. The term "bodymind" seems first to have been used by Candace Pert of the School of Medicine, Georgetown University, Washington, D.C., whose early research helped establish the highly complex and integrated physiochemical nature of human beings.
4. See Hart (1975) and (1998).
5. Thurman & Welch (2000), 21 and 138.
6. "Program" is referred to by Hart (1998) as "a sequence of steps or actions intended to achieve some 'goal,' which once built is stored in the brain and 'run off' repeatedly when ever need to achieve the same goal is perceived by the person" (p. 190).
7. Standardized attainment-testing systems used particularly in schools in the United States and the United Kingdom.
8. Johnston (1999).
9. Csikszentmihalyi (2000).
10. Gorman (1999).
11. Gregorc (1982).
12. Gardner (1999).
13. Thurman & Welch (2000), 206.
14. Adapted from Thurman & Welch (2000), 207.
15. Reviewed in Thurman & Welch (2000), 210–212. See also A. Kohn, *Punished by Rewards: The Trouble with Gold Stars, Incentive Plans, A's and Other Bribes* (New York: Houghton Mifflin, 1993).
16. Csikszentmihalyi (2000), 15.

17. Ibid., 49.
18. Elaborated in Thurman & Welch (2000), 195–199.
19. Hart (1998), 155.
20. Elaborated in Thurman & Welch (2000), 221–228.

Chapter 3

1. Storr (1991).
2. Further detailed information on neuropsychobiological development can be found in Thurman & Welch (2000), book 1, chapter 8.
3. Khan (1996), 163.
4. Thurman & Welch (2000), 166.
5. Ibid., 177.
6. Elliott (1995), 121.
7. Henningsson (1996).
8. Blacking (1987).
9. Oakley (1976).
10. Walker (1994).
11. Langer (1957), 222.
12. Cooke (1959), 15.
13. Reimer (1970).
14. Elliott (1995).
15. Turton & Durrant (2002).
16. Carried out by Evangelos Himonides as part of his graduate study in choral education at the University of Surrey Roehampton, 1997, and reported in Durrant & Himonides (1998).
17. Reimer (1970), 131.
18. Hiller (2001), 51, 54.

Chapter 4

1. Headington (1974).
2. Carse (1964).
3. Lang (1969).
4. Abraham (1990); Berlioz (1948); and Wagner (1870).
5. Kreuger (1958), 119.
6. Ibid., p. 123.
7. Berlioz (1948).
8. Berlioz did not take up conducting until 1835, when he wrote in his *Memoirs:* "The conductor must feel as I feel. They require a combination of irresistible verve and the utmost precision, a controlled vehemence, a dreamlike sensitivity, an almost morbid melancholy. . . . it is exceedingly painful to hear my works conducted by someone other than myself." A caricature by Doré (1850) shows Berlioz conducting with glowing enthusiasm (Berlioz conducting at the Société Philharmonique at the Jardin d'Hiver).
9. Meyer-Brown & Sadie (1989), 336.
10. Based on an account from Schünemann (1913) *Geschichte des Dirigiernes* (cited in Carse, 1964), in which Baron Grimm refers to the conductor of the Paris Opéra in 1753 as a "woodchopper," owing to the custom of beating time audibly.
11. Lang (1963), 964.

12. Schoenberg (1967), 26.
13. Robinson & Winold (1976).
14. Quoted in Schoenberg (1967), 28.
15. Fellowes (1969), 202.
16. Lebrecht (1991), 8.
    Lebrecht (1991), 11.
17. Quoted in E. Green (1981), preface.
18. Boult (1963), xiii.
19. Lebrecht (1991), 31.
20. Matheopoulos (1982), 276.
21. Carpenter (1992), 250.
22. Mark and Gary (1992).
23. Keene (1982).
24. Durrant (2001).

Chapter 5

1. Dostal (1993), 141.
2. Phelps, Ferrara, & Goolsby (1993), 109.
3. Ibid., 137.
4. Schon (1987), 25.
5. Polanyi (1983).
6. Broudy (1988).
7. Brown & McIntyre (1993), 19.
8. Collingwood (1938), 27.
9. Elbaz (1983), 15–21, 101.
10. Green & Gallwey (1987), 39.
11. Hart (1983).
12. Ibid., p. 164.
13. McCoy (1994). Emile-Jacques Dalcroze developed eurythmics, the theory that the natural rhythms of the body provide the origins of the rhythms of music, and he stressed the importance of rhythm and movement in musical training.

Chapter 6

1. Durrant (1996); (1998); (2000).
2. Cooke (1959).
3. Reference here is made to the Ricordi vocal score.
4. Gill (1992).
5. It should be made compulsory for all musicians (and aesthetic theorists) to listen to Britain's Radio 4 comic quiz program, *I'm Sorry I Haven't a Clue*. This consists of a series of bizarre, meaningless but brilliantly imaginative games. One frequently played requires each contestant to sing one song to the tune of another. An example might be to perform *Singing in the Rain* to the tune of *Edelweiss*. Try it! While it is remarkably hilarious (in the way that only British radio comedy can be), it does show how some songs fall apart without appropriate lyrics. One incidental feature to this game is the host Humphrey Lyttleton's ridiculously and intentionally complex explanation of its rules; this just goes to show how sometimes inadequate and superfluous instructional words can be—another important lesson for teachers and conductors!

6.	Crowe (1994).
7.	Hibbard (1994).
8.	Watkins (1986).
9.	Gumm (1991).

Chapter 7

1.	Mehrabian (1972).
2.	Hemsley (1998), 99. While he refers essentially to the solo singer, the advice has relevance for choral singers as well.
3.	Haasemann & Jordan (1991), 18.
4.	McNally (2001).
5.	Brewer (1997).
6.	Daugherty (2000).
7.	Gardner (1983); (1993); (1999).

Chapter 8

1.	Morris et al. (1979).
2.	More on this can be found in the movement pedagogy of Rudolph Laban; but for now it is about exploration of movement through time and space.

Chapter 9

1.	Welch (2001).
2.	Some examples of these approaches to learning songs were outlined in *Making Sense of Music* (1995), a textbook that I and Graham Welch wrote.
3.	Knight (2000), 146, 153.
4.	This list is based on a more expanded discussion in Durrant & Welch (1995).
5.	Welch & Murao (1994).
6.	Welch & Howard (2002).
7.	Cooksey (1992); see also Thurman & Welch (2000), book 4, chapter 4, and book 5, chapter 8.
8.	See Thurman & Welch (2000), book 4, chapter 5, and book 5, chapter 7 (by Lynne Gackle).
9.	Also reported in Durrant (2000).
10.	See Thurman & Welch (2000), book 4, chapter 6.
11.	Welch (1994).
12.	See Durrant & Welch (1995).

Chapter 10

1.	Lonis (1993).
2.	Bloom (1956).
3.	Strouse (1987).
4.	Swan (1987), 88.
5.	Elliott (1995).
6.	Donovan (1994).
7.	Ehmann & Haasemann (1981); Haaesemann & Jordan (1991).

8.   Decker & Kirk (1988).
9.   Rao (1993).

Chapter 11

1.   Apfelstadt (1997).
2.   Gardner (1995), 306.
3.   Carlow (2001).

BIBLIOGRAPHY

Abraham, G. (ed) (1990). "Romanticism 1830–1890." *New Oxford History of Music,* vol. 9, 56.

Apfelstadt, H. (1997). "Applying Leadership Models in Teaching Choral Conductors." *Choral Journal of the American Choral Directors' Association* 37 (8): 23–30.

Berlioz, H. (1948). *Grand Traité d'Instrumentation et d'Orchestration Modernes.* Translated by T. Front. New York.

Blacking, J. (1987). *A Common-Sense View of All Music.* New York: Cambridge University Press.

Bloom, B. (ed) (1956). *Taxonomy of Educational Objectives: The Classification of Educational Goals.* New York: Longman.

Boult, A. (1963). *Thoughts on Conducting.* London: Phoenix House.

Brewer, M. (1997). *Kick-Start Your Choir.* London: Faber Music.

Broudy, H. (1988). *The Uses of Schooling.* New York: Routledge.

Brown, S. & McIntyre, D. (1993). *Making Sense of Teaching.* Buckingham, England: Open University Press.

Carlow, R. (2001). "From Goodbye to Hello." Unpublished graduate assignment, University of Maryland.

Carse, A. (1964). *The History of Orchestration.* New York: Dover.

Collingwood, R. (1938). *The Principles of Art.* Oxford: Oxford University Press.

Colwell, R. (ed) (1992). *Handbook of Research on Music Teaching and Learning.* New York: Schirmer.

Cooke, D. (1959). *The Language of Music.* Oxford: Oxford University Press.

Cooksey, J. (1992). *Working with the Adolescent Voice.* St. Louis, MO: Concordia.

——— (2000). "Voice Transformation in Males Adolescents" and "Male Adolescent Transforming Voices: Voice Classification, Voice Skill Development and Music Literature Selection," in *Bodymind and Voice: Foundations of Voice Education.* Minneapolis, MN: The VoiceCare Network.

Crowe, D. (1994). "Error Detection Abilities of Conducting Students under Four Modes of Instrumental Score Study." Doctoral dissertation, University of Arizona.

Csikszentmihalyi, M. (2000). *Beyond Boredom and Anxiety: Experiencing Flow in Work and Play.* San Francisco: Jossey-Bass.

Daugherty, J. (2000). "Choir Spacing and Choral Sound: Physical, Pedagogical and Philosophical Dimensions," in *Sharing the Voices: The Phenomenon of Singing 2.* St. Johns, Memorial University of Newfoundland.

Decker, H. & Kirk, C. (1988). *Choral Conducting: Focus on Communication.* Englewood Cliffs, NJ: Prentice Hall.

Donovan A. (1994). "The Interaction of Personality Traits in Applied Music Teaching." Doctoral dissertation, University of Southern Mississippi.

Dostal, Robert J. (1993). "Time and Phenomenology in Husserl and Heidegger." In *The Cambridge Companion to Heidegger,* ed. Charles Guignon. Cambridge: Cambridge University Press.

Durrant, C. (1996). "Towards a Model of Effective Choral Conducting: Implications for Music Education, Musical Communication and Curriculum Development." Doctoral dissertation, University of Surrey.

――― (1998). "Developing a Choral Conducting Curriculum." *British Journal of Music Education* 15 (3): 303–316.

――― (2000). "Making Choral Rehearsing Seductive: Implications for Practice and Choral Education." *Research Studies in Music Education* 15: 40–49.

――― (2001). "The Genesis of Music Behaviour: Implications for Adolescent Music Education." *International Journal of Education* & *the Arts* 2: 5. Available at http://ijea.asu.edu/v2n5/

Durrant, C. & Himonides, E. (1998). "What makes people sing together? Socio-Psychological and Cross-Cultural Perspectives on the Choral Phenomenon." *International Journal of Music Education* 32: 61–71.

Durrant, C. & Welch, G. (1995). *Making Sense of Music: Foundations for Music Education.* London: Cassells.

Ehmann, W. & Haasemann, F. (1981). *Voice Building for Choirs.* Revised ed. Translated by B. Smith. Chapel Hill, NC: Hinshaw Music.

Elbaz, F. (1983). *Teacher Thinking: A Study of Practical Knowledge.* London: Croom Helm.

Elliott, D. J. (1995). *Music Matters: A New Philosophy of Music Education.* New York: Oxford University Press.

Farnsworth, P. R. (1954).*The Social Psychology of Music.* Ames: Iowa State University Press.

Fellowes, E. (1969). *English Cathedral Music.* 5th ed. London: Methuen.

Gackle, L. "Understanding Voice Transformation in Females Adolescents" and "Female Adolescent Transforming Voices: Voice Classification, Voice Skill Development and Music Literature Selection," in *Bodymind and Voice: Foundations of Voice Education.* Minneapolis, MN: The VoiceCare Network.

Gardner, H. (1983). *Frames of Mind: The Theory of Multiple Intelligences.* New York: Basic Books.

――― (1993). *Frames of Mind: The Theory of Multiple Intelligences.* New York: Basic Books.

――― (1995). *Leading Minds: An Anatomy of Leadership.* New York: Basic Books.

――― (1999). *Intelligence Reframed: Multiple Intelligences for the 21st Century.* New York: Basic Books.

Gill, R. (1992). "Understanding and Applying Aesthetics." *Choral Journal of the American Choral Directors' Association.* August 1992, 21–26.

Glenn, C. (ed) (1991). *In Quest of Answers: Interviews with American Choral Conductors.* Chapel Hill, NC: Hinshaw Music.

Goldman, R. F. (1966). "After Handel in Britain and America." In *Choral Music,* ed. A. Jacobs. Middlesex, England: Penguin.

Gorman, D. (1999). *Working with a Violinist: An Account of a Lesson.* Available at http://www.learningmethods.com/violin.htm

Green, B. & Gallwey, T. (1987). *The Inner Game of Music.* London: Pan Books.

Green, E. (1981). *The Modern Conductor.* Englewood Cliffs, NJ: Prentice Hall.

Gregorc, A. (1982). *An Adult's Guide to Style.* Columbia, CT: Gregorc.

Gross, R. (1996). *Psychology: The Science of Mind and Behaviour.* London: Hodder & Stoughton.

Gumm, A. (1991). "The Identification and Measurement of Music Teaching Styles." Doctoral dissertation, University of Utah.

Haasemann, F. & Jordan, J. (1991). *Group Vocal Technique.* Chapel Hill, NC: Hinshaw Music.

Hargreaves, D. J. (1986). *The Developmental Psychology of Music.* New York: Cambridge University Press.

Hargreaves, D. J. and North A. (eds) (1997). *The Social Psychology of Music.* New York: Oxford University Press.

Hart, L. (1975). *How the Brain Works.* New York: Basic Books.

——— (1998). *Human Brain and Human Learning.* Village of Oak Creak, AZ: Books for Educators.

Headington, C. (1974). *The Bodley Head History of Western Music.* London: Bodley Head.

Hemsley, T. (1998). *Singing and Imagination: A Human Approach to a Great Musical Tradition.* Oxford: Oxford University Press.

Henningsson, Ingemarr (1996). *Kor I Cirkel: Ett forum for indivduell och kollectiv utveckling* (Choir in the Circle: forum for individual and collective development). Rapport av ett FoU-projekt Frikyrkliga Studieforbundet, KFUK-KFUMs studieforbund, Sveriges Kyrkliga Studieforbund och Musikhogskolan, Gotesborg universitet.

Hibbard, T. (1994). "The Use of Movement as an Instructional Technique in Choral Rehearsals". Doctoral dissertation, University of Oregon.

Hiller, J. A. (2001). *Treatise on Vocal Performance and Ornamentation.* Translated and edited by Suzanne J. Beiken. Cambridge: Cambridge University Press.

Himonides, E. (1997). "What makes people sing collectively: Socio-psychological Perspectives on the Reasons Why People Sing Collectively." Graduate dissertation, University of Surrey Roehampton.

Inayat Khan, H. (1996). *The Mysticism of Sound and Music: The Sufi Teaching of Hazrat Inayat Khan.* Boston & London: Shambhala.

Johnston, V. (1999). *Why We Feel.* Reading, MS: Perseus Books.

Keene, A. (1982). *A History of Music Education in the United States.* Hanover and London: University Press of New England.

Knight, S. (2000). "Exploring a Cultural Myth: What adult non-singers may reveal about the nature of singing," in *Sharing the Voices: The Phenomenon of Singing 2.* St. Johns: Memorial University of Newfoundland.

Kohn, A. (1993). *Punished by Rewards: The Trouble with Gold Stars, Incentive Plans, A's and Other Bribes.* New York: Houghton Mifflin.

Kreuger, K. (1958). *The Way of the Conductor.* New York: Charles Scribner's Sons.

Lang, P. (1969). *Music in Western Civilization.* New York: Norton.

Langer, S. (1957). *Philosophy in a New Key.* Cambridge, MA: Harvard University Press.

Lebrecht, N. (1991). *The Maestro Myth.* London: Simon & Schuster.

Leong, S. (ed) (1997). *Music in Schools and Teacher Education: A Global Perspective.* School of Music, The University of Western Australia: ISME Commission Music in Schools and Teacher Education and Callaway International Resource Centre for Music Education.

Lonis, D. (1993). *Development and Application of a Model for the Teaching of Conducting Gestures.* Doctoral dissertation, University of Illinois Urbana Champaign.

Mac Laverty, B. (1997). *Grace Notes.* London: Jonathan Cape.

Mark, M. & Gary, C. (1992). *A History of American Music Education.* New York: Schirmer.

Matheopoulos, H. (1982). *Maestro: Encounters with Conductors of Today.* London: Hutchinson.

McCoy, C. (1994). "Eurythmics: Enhancing the Music-Body-Mind Connection in Conductor Training." *Choral Journal of the American Choral Directors' Association.* 35 (5): 21–28.

McNally, J. (2001). *Junior Choral Club.* London: Novello.

Mehrabian, A. (1972). *Nonverbal Communication.* Englewood Cliffs, NJ: Prentice Hall.

Meyer-Brown, H. & Sadie, S. (1989). *Performance Practice: Music after 1600.* London, England: MacMillan.

Morris, D., Collett, P., Marsh, P., O'Shaughnessy, M. (1979). *Gestures: Their Origins and Distribution.* London: Jonathan Cape.

Oakley, G. (1976). *The Devil's Music: A History of the Blues.* London: British Broadcasting Corporation.

Office for Standards in Education (1996). *The Annual Report of Her Majesty's Chief Inspector of Schools, 1994/5.* London: HMSO.

Phelps, R., Ferrara, L., Goolsby, T. (1993). *A Guide to Research in Music Education.* 4th ed. Metuchen, NJ & London: Scarecrow Press.

Polanyi, M. (1983). *The Tacit Dimension.* Gloucester, MA: Peter Smith.

Rao, D. (1993). *We Will Sing! Choral Music Experience for Classroom Choirs.* London & New York: Boosey & Hawkes.

Radocy, R. E. and Boyle, J. D. (1979). *Psychological Foundations of Musical Behavior.* Springfield, IL: Thomas.

Reimer, B. (1970). *A Philosophy of Music Education.* Engelwood Cliffs, NJ: Prentice Hall.

———— (1997). "Should there be a Universal Philosophy of Music Education?" *International Journal of Music Education* 29: 4–21.

Robinson, R. & Winold A. (1976). *The Choral Experience: Literature, Materials and Methods.* New York: Harper's College Press.

Schoenberg, H. (1967). *The Great Conductors.* New York: Simon & Schuster.

Schon, D. (1987). *Educating the Reflective Practitioner.* San Francisco: Jossey-Bass.

Shaw, S. & D'Angour, A. (1996). *The Art of Swimming.* Bath, England: Ashgrove.

Silbermann, A. (1963). *The Sociology of Music.* Translated by C. Stewart. London: Routledge & Kegan Paul.

Sloboda, J. A. (1985). *The Musical Mind: The Cognitive Psychology of Music.* Oxford: Clarendon.

Small, C. (1980). *Music, Society, and Education.* London: John Calder.

Stokes, M. (ed) (1994). *Ethnicity, Identity, and Music: The Musical Construction of Place.* Oxford: Berg.

Storr, A. (1991). "Music in Relation to the Self." *Journal of British Music Therapy* 5, (1): 5–13.

Strouse, L. (1987). *From Analysis to Gesture: A Comprehensive Approach to Score Preparation for the Conductor.* Doctoral dissertation, Ball State University, Indiana.

Swan, H. (1987). *Conscience of a Profession.* Chapel Hill, NC: Hinshaw Music.

Swanwick, K. (1988). *Music, Mind, and Education.* London: Routledge.

Thurman, L. & Welch, G. (2000). *Bodymind and Voice: Foundations of Voice Education.* Minneapolis, MN: The VoiceCare Network.

Turton, A. & Durrant, C. (2002). "A Study of Adults' Perceptions and Reflections on Their Singing Experience in Secondary School: Some Implications for Music Education." *British Journal of Music Education* 19 (1): 31–47.

Van Oyen, L. (1994). "The Effects of Two Instrumental Score Preparation Approaches on the Error Detection Ability of Student Conductors." Doctoral dissertation, University of Nebraska.

Wagner, R. (1870). *Uber das Dirigieren.*

Walker, R. (1994). "Will Karaoke Teach the World to Sing?" In *Onchi and Singing Development: A Cross-Cultural Perspective,* ed. Graham Welch and Tadahiro Murao. London: Roehampton Institute and David Fulton Publishers.

Watkins, R. (1986). "A Descriptive Study of High School Choral Directors' Use of Modeling, Metaphorical Language and Musical/Technical Language related to Student Attentiveness." Doctoral dissertation, University of Texas at Austin.

Welch, G. (2001). "The Misunderstanding of Music." Inaugural lecture. London: Institute of Education.

Welch, G. & Howard, D. (2002). "Gendered Voice in the Cathedral Choir." *Psychology of Music* 30: 103–120.

Welch, G. & Murao, T. (eds) (1994). *Onchi and Singing Development.* David Fulton Publishers, Advanced Studies in Music Education, Roehampton Institute, London.

Young, P. M. (1981). *The Choral Tradition.* New York: Norton.

INDEX